Seeing Through the Bull ...

The art of problem solving.

Bryan Beaty

ISBN: 1478176598
ISBN-13: 9781478176596

Contents

Dedication and Thanks

It isn't easy to live or work with someone who wants to solve all the world's problems. This is dedicated to those of you that have lived and worked with me over the years. Thanks for your patience, help, and ideas.

Special thanks to Shelley, Liz, Richard, Cheryl, Nita, Lori, and Eddy. You know why.

What got me into this mess ...

I like to eat. Not a lot, just enough to survive. A little over a year ago, I started my own business. Decomplexification, if you can believe the name, is just me as an independent consultant. If you have ever run your own company you know how difficult it can be to find new customers. Desperate for some improved marketing material, and for food, I asked my most faithful clients why they kept rehiring me.

Their response:

You see through the bull.

(It was actually a little more vulgar than that.) This wasn't the answer I was expecting. I was expecting something like:

- You are a technology expert.
- Your rates are lower than your competitor's.
- You work hard and never over-bill me.
- You're easy to work with.
- You have a great sense of humor.

"Seeing through bullshit" is difficult to market. How many people do a Google search for "Consulting to see through bullshit?" I felt hunger pains coming on.

The truth is, people rehire me because ...

I solve the problems my clients want solved, which are rarely the problems they hire me to solve.

They would hire me to determine how many new employees they needed and I would find that they didn't need new employees if they would make process changes. They would hire me to install a new email system and I would find that they only needed a few configuration changes. In short, I solve problems. More accurately, though, I solve the real problems.

The second thing they pointed out is that I have a problem-solving methodology. That was news to me. I never set off to be a problem solver. It was just something I learned to do through trial and error. In fact, I was a little sad people didn't love me because I was some sort of techno-genius.

What makes my methodology different is that my goal isn't only to identify the problem and solution but to get a solution implemented. You don't solve problems by identifying them. You solve problems by putting solutions that work in place. This requires two distinct activities. First you have to be able to identify the problem and solution. Second you have to be able to work with people to get the solution implemented. This book will help you do both.

I focus on the human side of problem solving because people are usually (part of) the problem. You can't look at a process flowchart and see that Bob and Sue hate each other and don't communicate well as a result. You can't look at an email server and see that users don't know how to organize their email. Being a good consultant, manager, information worker, business owner, or problem solver requires you to talk to people to solve problems. This book will help you identify problems and solutions but it goes further. It will help you get the solution implemented.

Finding the right solution doesn't solve problems. Implementing the right solution does.

PART I:
A LITTLE THEORY

You are notified that there is no coffee in the break room. You want your employees properly caffeinated so you order more. When it arrives, you take it to the break room and find a broken coffee maker and plenty of coffee. "Why didn't you tell me the coffee machine was broken?" you ask. They thought you knew.

This type of problem is common in business. You hear "There's no coffee in the break room" and assume you need to buy coffee. Employees, trying to avoid confrontation, will say "We are out of coffee" when they really mean "When are you going to fix the coffee machine?" Miscommunications and assumptions are common. Being out of coffee, although tragic, probably won't hurt your business. Someone spending $10,000 on something you don't need will. Of course, not spending money when you need to is just as bad ...

Why are we out of coffee anyway?

What if you had asked why there was no coffee in the break room? This simple question would have revealed the real problem. People often assume you know details you don't. Expecting them to give you every detail is a recipe for information overload. Expecting them to know which details you need and which details are irrelevant is a recipe for disaster.

Asking the right question at the right time is the right thing to do.

Sometimes you are just out of coffee

Yes, sometimes you are just out of coffee. You are told the break room is out of coffee, you ask why, and you find out Bob has been drinking more than his fair share due to a lack of sleep allegedly caused by a bad video game addiction. Apparently Sally also pours out the last inch of every pot because it is too strong. There's also a rumor the delivery person sneaks a cup when no one is looking. Unless you just like getting involved in minutia, there is no problem here to solve. It is just good to know you are spending money on coffee because people drink it.

Getting started

Problems come in all shapes and sizes. They can be so simple they are hardly worth considering or so complex it takes a team of people just to understand them. This book can be used to solve problems of any shape or size. You don't have to follow every step in the book for every problem you have. When you break a coffee cup all you need to do is replace it ... probably. When you break your business, you may need to do a little more thinking. Whenever you are faced with a problem to solve, use the portions of this book you need and skip the rest.

Secondly, I use the term *client* a lot. Since I am a consultant, I have clients. A client can be anybody, though. It could be your boss, your employees, or your co-workers. A client is anybody you are solving problems for. I also use the term *vendor* a lot. A vendor to me is someone that has a product or solution you need. It is usually an outside company but in some cases could be another person, department, consultant, etc., so don't get distracted by terminology.

Part I describes the mindset that makes the methodology, described in Part II and III, possible. If I were writing a book on being a doctor, Part I would be about having good bedside manners. Even the most knowledgeable doctors, lawyers, accountants, and problem solvers will struggle if they focus too much on the problem and too little on the client. It all starts with accepting a few difficult truths.

Universal Truths

Before we start learning how to solve problems, we must acknowledge a universal truth:

There are no perfect solutions.

Analytical people tend to believe that with enough effort, a perfect solution can be found to any problem. Everyone else believes that spending time thinking about problems is a waste. The truth is somewhere in the middle.

> *Have you read "Patriot Games" by Tom Clancy? In it, one of the bad guys tells the good guy the world is gray. For people like me who like to see things in black and white, gray just seems wrong. In reality, the world is gray. What happens when a solution costs more to implement than the problem costs if it is left alone? Much of the time, the best solution is too expensive or disruptive to implement. The world is gray.*

Would you like that fast, cheap, or right?

There is a saying in the software development world: "You can have it fast, cheap, or right. Choose any two." The point is that fast, cheap, and right are mutually exclusive. You can have two of the three but never all three. This is true for almost any solution. We don't want things to be uncontrollably expensive, completely wrong, or unbearably slow. Instead, we have to find a balance. Luckily, fast, cheap, and right are gray. You don't choose to have them or not, you choose how much of each you need.

> *A client wanted a network firewall installed between his servers and his workstations. The goal was to allow users to get to services they need like email but not be able to do anything else. Despite my concerns the client wanted this done fast and cheap. (They handed me a set of firewall rules instead of paying me to analyze the situation.) The firewall worked exactly as their rules were written but their employees could no longer access critical files. Administrators could no longer remote control the servers. Their solution was fast, cheap, and wrong. They ended up bringing me back to make adjustments. Their solution became less cheap, less fast, and more right.*

Balancing fast, cheap, and right is one of those topics that is both an academic subject worthy of a textbook and an art. We are going to focus on the art of balance in this book. Reading a textbook implies you can do something perfectly, which we have already accepted cannot be done. The art of balancing a solution starts with asking yourself a question:

Is it more important for my solution to be fast, cheap, or right?

Signs that your solution may be too fast

I don't have time to analyze the coffee consumption habits of my employees to create a predictive coffee ordering algorithm. I don't have time to ... Who has free time anyway? This is America where we work long hours and then read books about how to get even more done in our already overly-long work day. You may be too focused on fast if:

- Your solutions are consistently over budget.
- Your solutions rarely work as expected.
- You keep having to revisit decisions.

> *I once worked for an organization that decided to rename a business division to better describe what it did. When I heard the new name, I commented that the department's new acronym would spell a rather rude body function. Although they were upset that I had made such a rude observation, they decided not to use that name. Were it not for my "potty mind" this would have been a fast, cheap, and terribly wrong choice.*

Solving problems is like a race that is often lost by finishing first.

Signs that your solution may be too cheap

I am all for frugality. Not spending money keeps me from having to make as much money. Regardless of the benefits of frugality, it has a downside such as making your solution lengthy or wrong. You are (probably) being too cheap if:

• You assign additional work to an employee that is already fully utilized.
• You refuse to buy something that could solve your problem quickly and easily.
• You choose to use an existing item (such as software) instead of buying one that would work much better.
• You try to find ways of doing everything without spending additional money.
• You refuse to hire consultants when you don't have an in-house subject matter expert.
• You refuse to hire consultants when you don't have time to learn what they already know.

How many times have you visited a website and immediately left because the site was so poorly designed? I am always amazed when I find companies with websites that must drive away more business than they bring in. This is an example of being too cheap. It would be better to have no website than one that makes your company look bad. Hiring an expert to fix it would probably be a good idea.

Frugality is a constructive lack of spending. Being cheap is a destructive lack of spending.

Signs that your solution may be too right

Let's face it, nobody (hopefully) decides to create a solution that is wrong. Something is wrong to start with. Your solution is supposed to make it right. (Perhaps this is where the saying "Don't fix it if it ain't broken" comes from.) The danger with being too right is that you spend so much time and money solving a problem that you do more harm than good. Fixing a $10 problem by spending $100,000 is silly, but we sometimes get so wrapped up in solving the problem we lose perspective. We forget to balance fast, cheap, and right.

This creates the startling paradox that being right can be wrong.

I once worked with a client that wanted the new application my company was building to be perfect. We spent almost a year gathering requirements before we started building the system. During that year, their business changed, making our design invalid. By spending so much time getting things right, we ended up with a system that was wrong.

Getting to good enough

If there is no perfect solution, what kind of solution are we striving for? One with the right balance of fast, cheap, and right. The right balance usually means nobody finds the solution ideal. Budget-minded people will think it is too expensive. The people affected by the problem will think it doesn't solve all their problems. Managers may think it takes too long to implement. The goal is to find a solution that has the best balance between fast, cheap, and right. That makes the solution good enough.

I once had the pleasure of designing and building the first computer network for a mid-sized K-12 school district. I worked with teachers and administrators to gather requirements, which is a fancy way of saying I asked them what they wanted computers to do. The list I got was massive. When I calculated the cost to build such a network it was prohibitively expensive. At our next meeting I told them I could give them everything they wanted as long as every employee took a 30% pay cut. We decided instead to reduce our requirements (the "right" portion of the equation) which decreased costs to an acceptable level.

In the rare case I find a solution that seems fast, cheap, and right, I worry. This usually means something is going to go horribly wrong. Call me a pessimist but when something seems perfect, it usually means I don't understand it very well. Perfect-looking solutions are usually ones that I haven't researched enough. If everyone involved in a solution is happy, I start looking for problems.

Since everyone wants a solution that is fast, cheap, and right, and it is impossible to have a solution that is fast, cheap, and right ...

Everyone should be at least a little disappointed in your solution.

If you can learn to live with that, you are philosophically prepared to be a great problem solver.

Talk isn't cheap

You would think experts in logic would make the best problem solvers. That would be true if problems didn't involve people with emotions. People are driven by emotion. Don't believe me? There are dozens of fascinating books on the subject such as Predictably Irrational by Dan Ariely (Harper Perennial; 2010) or Freakonomics by Steven Levitt and Stephen Dubner (William Morrow Paperbacks; 2009). Put simply ...

People are irrational.

Feelings are important

Problem solving is a logical (rational) process. People are irrational. (Irrational is defined as not-logical. Being irrational is being human.) When you add irrational people to a rational process you get strange results. You cannot force people to be rational nor can you use an irrational process to solve problems. Irrational behavior makes problem solving difficult.

When I solve problems for clients, I interview a lot of people and ask a lot of questions. I am thinking "How can I make things better for these people?" They are thinking "The boss hired some stranger to make things more efficient. That must mean the boss thinks I am inefficient and unable to make things better myself. The consultant is going to justify his invoice by finding ways of saving money like firing me! My job is going to be eliminated! My kids won't go to college! The sky is falling!" (This is only a slight exaggeration.) People get scared when you start asking questions. This is both irrational and unavoidable.

Being questioned terrifies most people.

To be a good problem solver:

You must help people feel good about what you are doing.

You don't have to be a counselor or psychologist but you do need to be a great communicator.

> *Both my mom and dad were ministers, and they taught me a lot about communication. They were trained to calm people down, make them feel better, be compassionate, etc. They used those techniques on me and I use them when I work. All of the logical problem-solving skills I have would be useless if I couldn't get people to trust me.*

Are you a good communicator?

Imagine this common scene: I am called in by a CEO to meet with employees regarding some process he feels is too slow, expensive, or erratic. I sit in on a department meeting and the CEO goes through each person's job and tells me what they do and how they manage their part of the process. After telling me how everything works the CEO asks his employees if he forgot anything or has anything wrong. I hear nothing but crickets chirping. Wow, one quick meeting and I know everything I need to know: The CEO is a terrible communicator.

When I see employees brainstorming solutions with the boss, contradicting him politely when he makes errors, disagreeing, arguing professionally, or other similarly open activities, I know the boss listens to his employees and they feel trusted to speak their mind. I learn how things actually work in meetings like these.

When I see employees sitting mute while the boss tells me how the company works, I know the boss expects people to do what he says. These employees will say what the boss expects them to say. I learn how the boss assumes things work in meetings like these.

Signs you probably communicate well:

- Your employees bring you new ideas.
- You hear when your employees are happy or frustrated with something they are doing.
- Employees let you know when you make a mistake.
- Employees question you in meetings.

Signs you probably communicate poorly:

- Employees do exactly what you say, even when it leads to disaster.
- Nobody asks you questions.
- You make mistakes and nobody corrects you.

If you cannot communicate well, you are going to have a hard time solving problems.

The good news is, by using a problem-solving process you will be forced to interact with and listen to your employees. You may be able to build a more open, honest, and beneficial relationship. If this is simply not something you can or wish to do, hire a consultant that is a good communicator to help.

Why people lie

When the boss starts asking questions or calls in a consultant, one thing is certain. Something is about to change.

People hate change.

One of the worst changes people can imagine is losing their job. Although their fears might be irrational, their response won't be. You will get the answers they think will keep them employed with as little change as possible. They don't do this maliciously. They just want to keep their jobs. (And if possible, keep them as they are.)

People will lie to prevent change.

To be fair, I am being blunt to the point of rudeness. People rarely lie on purpose. In their mind they think they are protecting the company's reputation, their boss's reputation, or some other equally noble cause when they present information in an overly positive light. It may not be an outright lie to spin the facts into something they feel comfortable presenting, but it isn't helpful to you when you are trying to solve problems.

People don't know they are lying.

Even worse, people think they are being helpful when they lie.

Preventing lies

I get hired to solve problems. Most of those problems have resulted in people being overworked or overstressed. In all my years of consulting, I have learned one absolute truth:

People love to talk about how much work they do.

You have to be honest with the people you interview. When people are nervous, their bullshit detectors go into hyperactive mode and if you sound disingenuous, they are going to clam up like a wax figure.

Knowing this, I ask for information about each employee I am going to interview. I need to know who they are, what their job is, what they do best, and most importantly, how this problem directly affects them. I like to be able to walk into an office and say "Hi, I'm Bryan and I want you to help me better understand how the <problem process/system> works. I hear you are the resident expert on <what you do best.> I have also heard this is a real pain for you because ..."

This is never a prepared speech because that sets off bullshit detectors. I just work these items into the first few minutes of conversation. I need people to know that their boss told me good things about them and the boss knows their job is a pain because of the problems I am here to solve. I also like to throw in the true statement that I am here to try to make their life at work more pleasant.

People need to hear they are appreciated and can safely complain about their jobs.

Once they lose (most of) their fear, they start telling me how the company really works. The difference between how the boss thinks his company works and how it really works is always amazing.

The importance of being trusted by people cannot be overstated.

Lastly, as a consultant, I never throw people under the bus. It isn't uncommon for me to find that the person that hired me is part of the real problem. When I have to go back to the CEO or manager that hired me and explain that their disorganized, chaotic, micro-manager procedures are part of the problem, they sometimes want to know who said such things about them. I never reveal my sources.

Employees won't be honest if they are afraid of retaliation.

If you are trying to solve problems in your own company, you may find it difficult to get honest feedback from your employees. No matter how personable you are, people rarely feel comfortable criticizing you directly.

People don't like conflict.

There are many great books out there on building teams that communicate well. One of my favorites is "The Five Dysfunctions of a Team" by Patrick Lencioni.

> *I was once hired to determine if more employees needed to be added to a growing company. The CEO was concerned that no matter how many hours everyone worked, there was always more to do. While interviewing employees I learned that everyone really loved the CEO. They loved her so much they wouldn't tell her that she was the reason they couldn't get the work done. It seemed the CEO had to approve every transaction they processed. This made the CEO a bottleneck which prevented everyone else from being able to do their job. I worked with the CEO to create new rules which allowed employees to approve all*

but the most expensive transactions. (This is something she wanted to put in place, anyway.) This reduced the workload on the CEO, eliminated the backlog, and kept her from wasting money on new employees. A little truth goes a long way.

Machines can't talk ... yet.

If you work in a technical field, such as information technology, you might be asking yourself why you would need to communicate with people at all. If you are having a problem with a computer, it isn't like you will be talking to the actual machine.

True ... but false. In my experience, many technical failures come about after someone did something. Maybe someone patched the server, installed new software, added hardware and then mysteriously, the server started acting weird. Many people get defensive or minimize what they did because they don't want to be responsible for the problem. Communicating under these circumstances is very challenging.

> *I was called in to fix a Microsoft Exchange email system that had stopped working. The system was completely hosed. (That's the technical term for very messed up.) I asked if any changes had been made to the system and was assured nobody had touched it.*
>
> *After many expensive hours of work, I found that someone had installed a virus scanner on the system that wasn't designed to work with Microsoft Exchange. The first time an email came in with a virus, the virus scanner essentially deleted the entire email system database. This was an easy fix but it would have taken only minutes to find had someone admitted to installing the virus scanner in the first place.*

So, was it their fault for not admitting what they had done, or my fault for asking the question in a way that sounded accusatory?

Finding Fault

Fault is irrelevant. Finding fault doesn't solve anything.

Business, technology, and almost everything else changes daily, while processes tend to stay the same. People don't like to change despite the fact that everything around them is changing. The result is usually a process firmly grounded on the way things used to be. A friend of mine in the military once told me "The military is 200 years of tradition uninterrupted by progress." Most businesses I work with haven't been in business for 200 years, but many remain uninterrupted by progress.

Although it might sound like I am making fun of companies for not changing, I am not. The real point is that time and changes outside the business are at fault for many of the problems I run into. When I explain to people that a lot has changed since they started doing things a certain way and that we are trying to find ways of using new tools to help them, they don't feel like I am on a witch hunt.

If nothing ever changed, there wouldn't be many problems.

Being two people

Returning to a common theme in this book, finding balance is the key to problem solving. A great problem solver has to find the right balance between communicating with people and analyzing data. The best analyst will fail if the data they have is incomplete. The best communicator will fail if they don't know how to work through the data. Communication and analytical skills are not mutually exclusive, but most people find one to be naturally easy and the other to be foreign and difficult.

You either have to get good at both, or work with someone else that has the skills you are still developing.

Knowing what you don't know

The word research used to scare the hell out of me. In high school there was nothing more ominous than a research paper. That meant hours in the library looking through old dusty books trying to find information I didn't care about. Luckily for all of us, this is not the type of research I am talking about.

Research, in the context of problem solving, is learning what you are assuming. Since most people tend to think they know everything about their company, this is a step that is often overlooked or neglected.

Getting real

Another universal truth:

You are not omniscient.

You may have started the company, designed every process, trained every employee, and have an IQ of 190 but you still don't know what is really happening. Put simply, your employees do the work you don't do. They know more about it than you. Things have changed since you trained them. They do things their way, not your way.

Everything changes.

Understanding that you do not know everything is a critical step in becoming a great problem solver.

> I was a fourth grade teacher ... for two years. I won't get on my soapbox about education but trust me, the job is hard. What was most frustrating was the number of reports I had to fill out. I was forever providing stats on everything from attendance to reading levels. Sometimes I felt I spent more time compiling reports than I did

teaching. I was sure nobody in the administration building had a clue to the amount of work they were making teachers do.

Fast forward a few years and I worked as the IT manager for a school district. I was amazed at how many reports I had to ask teachers to generate so I could get funding for their technology, programs, and positions. If the teachers didn't supply the data, I couldn't get the grants that gave them the tools they needed. I was sure the state and federal legislature had no idea of the amount of work they were making school administrators do,

I have yet to run for elected office, and have no plans to try, but I am sure those elected want the reports to show the voters how their legislation has improved schools. I seriously doubt they have any idea how much paperwork they create and how much time is spent generating it.

What seems clear to me is that the people on one end of any process have very little knowledge about how the people on the other end of the process do their jobs. Understanding only one side of a process is like trying to understand a book while reading only the even-numbered pages.

Don't make an ASS out of U and ME

Assume nothing. That's the mindset required to solve problems. The trouble is, everyone assumes something. You assume your employees are telling you what you need to know. They assume you already know something. The vendors that gave them their information assume you know something. The software developer that wrote the application you use to analyze your data assumed you knew something. We are surrounded by assumptions. It isn't wrong to make decisions based on assumptions as long as you know they are assumptions ... but we usually don't know.

A client started a new service a few months prior to hiring me to speed up their billing process. They made money on every transaction and wanted to increase the number of transactions they were processing. I learned they had months of backlogged paperwork that still needed to be processed. This meant they didn't actually know if the new service was profitable or not. We made the backlog a priority and learned that they lost money on every transaction. Since spending money to lose money is a bad idea, they chose to shut the new service down and focus on the profitable side of the company.

The only assumption you should make is that you will be dealing with assumptions.

Seriously, don't be an ass

Not making assumptions is critical but so is winning trust. In order to not make assumptions, you have to ask more questions of people. In order to win trust you have to keep people from feeling like they are being interrogated. Later we will talk more about how to do this. For now, just realize the importance of getting the information you need without alienating the people that have the information.

People don't like to be interrogated.

The good, the bad, and the ethical

I am going to assume you know right from wrong. I will further assume you prefer an ethical solution. If on the other hand you are self-centered and don't mind breaking the law or hurting others when it suits you, put this book down and start looking for a job as a dictator or mob boss.

You can't be a good problem solver if you only care about yourself.

What do you do when solving a problem makes your life more difficult? Perhaps by doing something you hate you can save someone else's job. What is the ethical thing to do?

I think we have seen plenty of unethical behavior lately. Consider the collapse of the auto industry and the expensive government bail-outs that followed. I am no expert but I believe there was a plenty of unethical behavior that led to those events. Management, many years ago, tried to underpay workers, which led to the formation of unions. Unions focused solely on the well-being of their members at the expense of the auto companies. Management failed to control costs. Employees failed to control costs. Too much focus on the self and too little focus on the well-being of the company led to a collapse.

What about the banking industry? People were rewarded for "extreme" profit. This led to more creative and dangerous financial schemes. Stockholders demanded huge profits and were happy to get them ... and blindly assumed their unrealistic expectations wouldn't lead to unethical behavior. Executives wanted to keep their jobs and huge salaries and overlooked the questionable ethics of some of their employees. Employees wanted to move up the corporate ladder and made bad decisions. Too much focus on the self and too little on the good of the company and its clients led to a horrific collapse and bailout.

I am a geek and genetically disposed to love Star Trek. I am analytical and I love the character Spock. Vulcans have a saying which I appreciate: "The needs of the many outweigh the needs of the few or the one." Put in work terms, the needs of the company outweigh your needs. You were hired to make the company prosper. You are compensated for whatever inconvenience that causes you.

When solving problems, your solution should be the one that is best for the company, regardless of how it affects you.

I realized a client was likely to be out of business in a few years. Changes in regulations made it impossible to be profitable. I brought this up and within a few hours we decided to shut the company down. Although this was the right decision, I lost one of my biggest clients. I almost put myself out of business by doing what was right for my client. Over time though, that client recommended me to everyone she knew. Having a reputation for being ethical, even at your own expense, is marketable. (Just as a disclaimer, let me point out that we decided to shut the company down while it was in a position to help the employees find new jobs instead of waiting until they simply couldn't make payroll.)

Ethics doesn't make you a sucker

Ethics is a two-way street. You should be doing what is best for the company but not at an unreasonable personal expense.

When I started in IT I worked for organizations that had very little money. I was always shorthanded. I had the choice between working 80-hour weeks or lowering everyone's expectations of what I could accomplish. I chose to lower expectations. I was rightfully unwilling to do the work of two people. I wanted the organization to succeed but not at my personal expense. They ended up agreeing and hiring more people.

Ethics is the corporate version of a team sport. If you want to win, you need the whole team to play.

Ethics is something you possess as an individual, but for it to be effective, you have to work for a company that has an ethical culture. If you work for a company that is perfectly happy to shaft customers, it will be perfectly happy to shaft you. When I find myself employed by a company with a culture of questionable ethics, the only problem I solve is finding myself another job.

> *One of the consulting companies I worked for became more desperate for sales and started hiring sales people with questionable ethics. They were constantly asking me to recommend unnecessary products to customers. This would have violated the trust I had built with my clients and was unethical. I found a new job.*

You are not a judge ... unless you are.

Unless you are a judge, you aren't. It is likely you will learn a lot about the people you work with. It is easy to judge them, but doing so is counterproductive. As I have said many times before, you will not be able to solve problems if people don't trust you. If people feel you are judging them, they will not trust you.

People don't like being judged.

Your job is to fix a problem, not point out who made what mistake. Consider how people will react if you throw them under the bus in your report. By pointing out that someone makes a lot of mistakes, you make them hostile to your proposed solution. They will find a way to pay you back. It is a lose-lose scenario.

If I find that an employee makes a lot of mistakes, I recommend additional training. That's a nice way of letting the boss know there is a problem without saying anything bad about the employee. I might say something like "There seems to be a lot of confusion about how to do ... ." Statements like these are about the job or process, not about the actual employee.

Tell the truth

As an adult you know you are supposed to tell the truth, but there are times when it is painful and difficult to do so.

> *One of my clients hired her daughter to work with her. The daughter, just out of high school, lacked professional experience. She occasionally said or did things that the other employees felt were inappropriate in a professional environment. This made all the employees uncomfortable but nobody said anything about it. When I learned of this, I pointed out some of the unprofessional conduct to my client, who quickly resolved the issue. (We all need a little training when we are new to the workforce.)*

What I find most often is people omit the truth as opposed to lying. This goes back to people not liking conflict. When you are problem solving you will find many omitted truths. Finding ways of getting them in the open can be difficult but is another critical component to problem solving.

People omit the truth when it is uncomfortable.

Don't break the law.

For those of you willing to break laws, you are the problem. Solve it by turning yourself in to the authorities. For the rest of us, not breaking the law is obvious. What is less obvious is the need to follow best practices, standards, or company policies.

> *I hired a consultant to help customize software for my company. I quickly realized he did not have a virus scanner on his laptop which he had connected to our network. I never rehired him. Any technical consultant willing to put their client's network at risk by not following the most basic and well know security precautions isn't anyone I will do business with. He might have been the best developer in the history of developers but I lost*

faith in him because he didn't follow well known and established best practices.

When working with clients, I make it a point to show them how I follow best practices. I want them to see I am willing to practice what I preach. This builds trust and respect. By now, you should be thinking to yourself... "Ah, trust and respect, critical components of problem solving."

Think outside the box ... except when you shouldn't

I love thinking outside the box but there are times when it is inappropriate. When I am hired, I am asked to fix a specific problem. That's my box. What happens when I find another completely unrelated problem? That's another box. Unless the two boxes are connected in such a way that I have to solve both in order to solve one, I need to leave box two alone. In this case, it literally isn't my problem. Similarly, as a manager, I am hired to manage my department. Trying to solve problems for other managers without being asked is a recipe for conflict.

Solve what you were hired to solve.

It is ethical and appropriate to make your employer aware of other problems you find but you need to be careful. If you make it look like the company is falling apart by finding dozens of unrelated problems people will stop listening to you. You will either be seen as Chicken Little (The sky is falling!) or as someone fishing for more business.

Nobody likes working with Chicken Little.

Too much change can be as bad as none

When a company has dozens of major process problems, fixing them all at once can be as bad as fixing nothing. They have probably operated with these problems for years. Employees know how to work with or around these problems. Fixing too much at once leads to confusion and unexpected consequences. This leads to another startling paradox:

You can break a company by fixing it.

When implementing multiple changes, it may be best to fully implement one before proceeding to the next.

Thinking about thinking

I usually find one of two problems when I am hired by a client. They either ignored a problem until it grew into something horrific or they spent so much time thinking about it they couldn't decide what to do. Either scenario guarantees the problem will continue on and on ... . Learning to recognize these situations is key to being a great problem solver.

Analysis Paralysis

For those of us that are analytical, this is a common problem. We analyze a situation, come up with dozens of probable scenarios, and create solutions with unique pros and cons. In the end, our analysis is a waste because we can't decide which is the best solution. Hence the term "analysis paralysis."

Overanalyzing situations will make you an ineffective manager.

Symptoms of analysis paralysis usually include thoughts such as:

- I can't decide.
- If I do this, that will happen but if I do that, this will happen.
- This isn't a perfect solution.
- I need to rethink this.

If you find yourself re-thinking a problem looking for a better solution that you just can't seem to find, it may be time to recognize and accept that there is no perfect solution.

If you can't find a better solution, it might be because there isn't one.

Occasionally you may find that doing nothing is the best choice. As the old saying goes, the cure may be worse than the disease. Sometimes you just have to admit that the solutions are too expensive or cumbersome to justify, and that living with the problem is the best choice.

> *I can think of dozens (perhaps hundreds) of times I have had analysis paralysis. It wasn't easy for me to learn that there wasn't a perfect solution. Right now I am overwhelmed by the numerous examples I could provide in this book. Do I use another technology example? Do I use a management example? Which would be best? How many of each type of example do I already have in the book? Will that change in editing? I can't decide! I need to re-think this!*

It's hard to write a book when you overanalyze each sentence.

Ignorance isn't bliss

The opposite end of the analysis spectrum is pure ignorance. Ignorance comes in two flavors: intentional and unintentional.

Intentional ignorance is a choice. Perhaps someone finds computers baffling so they intentionally learn nothing about them. They just want them to work and they use them without every trying to understand them. This usually results in an un-patched unprotected computer with dozens of viruses, slow hard drives, and other frustrating problems.

> *I once knew someone that avoided anything related to automotive maintenance and was really upset when the engine seized up. To them, it was just another example of cars being unreliable. The mechanic found that the*

engine had never had an oil change. Even worse, there wasn't any oil left in the engine.

Unintentional ignorance is different, and harder to recognize, because we think we are doing the right thing when we aren't. When I started my consulting practice I had to make a lot of decisions. What kind of corporation do I form? How do I pay myself? What records do I keep? What software do I use? What insurance does the business need? To the best of my knowledge I made good choices, but a subject matter expert, such as a lawyer or insurance agent, might instantly recognize critical mistakes I have made.

> *I got a call from a company that had been backing up a critical database to tape every night without fail. When their server died, they were able to restore their database but it was damaged and could not be used. They didn't know the backup software they used wasn't designed to back up a live database. An expert would have instantly recognized this problem.*

What we don't know will almost certainly hurt us.

Balance, Balance, Balance

The amount of time or money you spend on a problem should be proportional to the amount of pain it causes or could cause. Learning to recognize when you are spending too much or too little time on a problem requires that you be self-aware. You have to know when you are overdoing it or ignoring something. You may need to retrain your brain to recognize these situations.

When I am retraining my brain, I find that simplicity and repetition are key elements. It may be as simple as putting a sticky note on your monitor that says "Should I be thinking more or less about this?" Every time you find yourself making a decision, ask yourself that question.

If you hate the subject matter, like IT, legal, or HR, find someone else to deal with it for you. If you love the subject matter too much, start calculating how much you are thinking about the problem and what it is costing the company in order to see if it is really worth your time.

The goal is to have just enough information to make a good decision.

Solve problems like a rock star

Solving a problem is half the battle. Getting people to buy into your solution is the other half. If you have kids this is easy to understand. You tell them what they should do and they do what they want. It can be the same at work.

As I have stated before, people don't like change. Businesses are collections of people. There seems to be some universal law where the resistance to change grows exponentially along with the number of employees, especially managers, involved.

Resistance to new ideas grows with the number of people involved.

You not only have to be trusted to get the information you need out of people, but you also have to be trusted to give solutions back. That is the problem solver's double-edged sword.

They don't get it

You walk into a meeting with the best solution you have ever come up with. You have spent months working on this brilliant idea. You have 10 minutes to present your findings and propose a solution. At the end of the meeting people don't seem to grasp why they all need to change. At the end of the day everyone agrees to think about it, which essentially means your idea is dead. What went wrong?

One common assumption people make when presenting solutions is that everyone already understands the problem. This is rarely true.

Don't assume everyone understands or even believes in the problem.

While you spent months thinking about the problem, everyone else was doing their job ... and not thinking about the problem. It is hard to convey all the reasoning and logic behind a solution in a short presentation. It is even harder to keep people awake in a long detailed presentation. If your presentation is the first time people have heard about your ideas, you will have a hard time selling your solution.

Presenting a solution is just the tip of the iceberg.

You are a politician ... sorry.

I hate to admit it but in business, politics is a way of life. No matter how large or small your company, if you work with other people, there is politics. We could call it a difference of opinion or philosophy but that sounds too fluffy for the steaming pile of bull it really is. Politics is difficult. Politics is frustrating. Politics is unavoidable.

Problem solvers that can't get their solutions implemented don't solve anything.

The larger the problem I am working on, the more time I spend politicking.

Make it their problem.

The best way I know to get people behind my solutions is to help them realize they have a problem. This is what I call politicking. Remember to use your excellent communication skills. Telling someone they have a problem only you can solve is likely to offend and build animosity. Asking someone if they are as frustrated as you are about a problem and then discussing possible solutions builds camaraderie. In the end, if the problem doesn't affect them somehow, they won't be motivated to help you.

People don't care about your problems. They have their own.

Make it their solution

Once you have helped everyone realize how this problem affects them, ask them if they think your idea would work or if there is anything that could be done different or better. If they think they helped create the solution, they will be more likely to support it. Make sure you share the credit when people help you. It make those that help you feel good, as well as letting everyone else know this was a team effort.

Solutions that have the support of all the stakeholders are easy to get approved.

Teach "good enough"

Not everyone understands getting to good enough. It is common for people to try to find better solutions than the ones I have come up with. During my politicking sessions, I spend a lot of time saying things like "I like that idea too but I can't find a way to make it cost effective." Notice that I "like" the idea making them feel good, while also making them focus on the balance between cheap, fast, and right.

> *A lot of growing small businesses ask me to install their first server. They have usually spent years trying to share files via email and are ready to make things more efficient. Since they are willing to spend money and want a fast solution it is hard to talk them out of a server. Instead I talk to them about how much time and effort is required to manage a server. It usually doesn't take long for them*

to realize that a server would be one more thing they have to deal with every day. We then look for solutions that are better suited for their business.

Look at the bright side

Sometimes the idea of good enough isn't well received. This is especially true when your solution will be compared to a competitor's solution. (The competitor could be another department in your company or another company entirely.)

People want to be viewed as successful ... not good enough.

On a personal note, I sometimes get frustrated when I visit peers that live in houses and drive cars far more expensive than mine. I work as hard and earn as much as they do but they seem to be doing so much better. I then realize they have gigantic mortgage and car payments while I do not. Not having payments allowed me to take the time to start my own business. One "solution" makes someone look successful, while the other provides more balance.

This isn't to say that you should never have the best-looking solution. There are times when it is important to do so. Again, we are striving for balance. We don't want this solution to cost so much that we can't implement other solutions to other problem in the future.

Don't mortgage tomorrow to pay for today.

Don't Lie

Once you feel you have enough support from stakeholders to present your solution to management, schedule your presentation. It is hard to provide sage advice about how best to present to managers since they are all different. Some like quick simple presentations. Others want all the details. As a general rule I keep my presentations or proposals short and leave plenty of time to answer questions. Regardless of what you do, don't lie.

Presenting facts you know to be wrong is an obvious lie. Presenting assumptions or estimates as if they are facts is also a lie. One of the biggest mistakes I see people make while presenting solutions is spouting huge ROI, TCO, or other cost based estimates to managers. Unless you have indisputable proof that your numbers are accurate, keep them to yourself. Inflated cost or savings estimates put manager's bullshit detectors on full alert. Worse is that unrealistic estimates make people question the validity of your solution. This is what I call overselling a solution. It is common and a recipe for failure.

If you want people to trust you, don't bullshit them.

A vendor tried to sell me a fax solution based on ROI calculations they performed. They calculated the cost of my employees walking to and from the fax machine. "Look how much you will save with our solution!" they said. When I looked at the numbers I asked them how keeping people from walking to the fax machine would result in savings. I still have to pay them. In reality, I would only have saved money if I fired someone. For a very large company receiving or sending thousands of faxes hourly, these calculations would have been appropriate. For my company of 50 with maybe 10 faxes arriving per day, it was a joke. Although I liked the solution, I didn't feel I could trust the company to accurately represent what the software could do. I didn't buy it.

When making your presentation, stick to facts you can defend. I always spell out hard costs or saving. These are costs or savings you can clearly define such as the purchase cost of a server, software, or exercise bike. For example, I might say "Our existing software costs $15,000 per year while this new solution will cost $10,000 per year." Then I move on to soft costs or savings. I might say something like "Although it is impossible to accurately estimate the benefit of using the new software, I believe we will see improved productivity and morale from the employees using it." Use specific details when possible.

Check your references.

When I am presenting solutions that are either products or services, I am often asked "Who else has done this?" Being able to name companies, departments, or people that have successfully done what you are proposing can help get your solution approved. This step isn't always necessary but is worth considering before every presentation.

Present the way they want

Some companies want information to be formally presented while others want to just sit down and informally discuss something. Some people think meetings are for formal information sharing while others think of them as discussion time. Work with whatever culture you have. Don't try to change company culture while you are presenting a solution.

> *I worked for a company once where the culture considered it rude to bring up items in meetings unless they had been discussed privately first. This made it impossible to brainstorm. I kept trying to change the culture by brainstorming in meetings. In the end I was unsuccessful in changing the culture. Worse yet, I made upper management hostile to my ideas which seriously limited my effectiveness. This was a very unpleasant experience which might have been avoided had I adjusted to the culture.*

Just because you don't like it, doesn't mean it needs to be fixed.

PART II:
WHAT'S YOUR (REAL) PROBLEM?

Ensure that what clients are asking for will actually work.

What happens in many cases is that they are trying to treat a symptom instead of a problem. Once I point this out, they usually don't need the solution they thought they needed, and thus, they don't need me. So much for eating.

> *I was called to help a client implement a paperless office. They wanted a server, document scanner, and software that would allow them to scan, organize, and find their documents quickly and easily. The client believed they lacked the technology to properly organize their documents. When I arrived at their office, I saw paper. I would not be exaggerating if I said mountains of paper. Every surface was covered in piles of paper. The floor had piles of paper and they had to create trails to their desks. I have never seen so much paper.*

So what is the problem? They obviously have a lot of paper. Do they need it all? Are they required to keep it for legal reason? Has the fire marshal ever been here? What I really need to know is WHY they have so much paper lying around.

> *During my interview with the client it became clear that they did not have a process for managing paper. When the mail arrived, they just threw it down somewhere. Important documents went into piles closer to a desk. Other stuff was put into the closest "to be filed" pile. They have empty filing cabinets and no system for organizing files. They are pilers, not filers. When asked why they didn't file all this paper, they said they didn't have time.*

So what's a consultant to do? I could have sold them the server, scanner, and software. I would have made money by training them how to use it. I could have walked away happy in the knowledge that I sold them what they asked for ... but then there would have been the guilt.

I would have only treated a symptom. Put simply, they were disorganized. Technology, in and of itself, does nothing to help people organize. Technology can only speed up an organized system. Had I done this, they would have cleared a space for the scanner, scanned a dozen documents, and then started pilling paper on top of it. In all probability, they would have been pissed at me for selling them a solution that was so slow and cumbersome.

> *While looking at their problem, trying not to be killed by a paper avalanche, and thinking about their proposed solution, I realize I can't do this job. They don't have time to open the mail, throw away the junk, open a desk drawer, flip to the correct folder, and drop the paper in it. How would they possibly have time to open the mail, throw away the trash, scan the rest, properly classify the files, and save them to the correct digital folder? They don't even have time to open the mail and throw away the trash!*

I turned down the job. The good news is that I lost three pounds in the ensuing "no income" diet. Perhaps that could be my next book! "How to Lose Weight by Consulting."

> *Instead of installing a scanner, I recommended they create a process for dealing with paper. Once that was done, I would be able to better help them with their technology. They understood and agreed with my findings, but I never heard from them again.*

Sometimes you have to tell people what they don't want to hear.

Don't confuse this story with more theory on ethics. Ethics keeps me from treating symptoms like problems. What will make you valuable to your employer or client isn't just ethics, it is the ability to see through symptoms to the real problem.

Methodology or madness?

While talking to my clients, they compliment my methodology for solving problems. They made it sound like I had some formal or magical system.

That was news to me.

When outlining this book though I started to realize I did have a methodology. It was just something I had created from trial and error. It was something I did out of habit and experience. I didn't use a formal logic system such as those documented on <u>Wikipedia</u>. I used my own combination of techniques which helped me determine what the real problem was, and then came up with a solution that was good enough.

As I continued to write I started breaking down my methodology into sections. First I communicate with people to better understand the problem. Then I research what I learned so far. I analyze anything that needs more thought. Lastly, I present my findings. You might be interested to know that I had also just settled on the name of the book as well. Do you see the connection yet?

Yes, I have developed the CRAP methodology while writing a book named Seeing Through the Bull. I'm so ... proud.

Don't ignore bizarre ideas. Just because they seem weird doesn't mean they aren't right.

I can't say the CRAP methodology is scientifically proven to be the best problem-solving technique in the known universe but it works for me and is very memorable. (I bet you will never forget Communicate, Research, Analyze, and Present.) The jokes about this are so numerous and obvious, I'll just leave them out.

Moving on ...

Cutting the CRAP

Despite the fact that I am writing a book on how to solve problems, there isn't a one-size-fits-all way to go about it. The CRAP methodology is scalable, meaning you only use what you need. Additionally it isn't linear, meaning that you don't work through it like a flowchart. For example, there are times where I might do some analysis after communicating. (That would have made this the CARP methodology, and how memorable would that have been?)

As you read through this section realize it isn't the order of the steps that matter. What matters is ensuring you have considered all the steps before you draw any conclusions. Secondly, you may repeat each step dozens of times as you work though a problem. The first time I "cut through the CRAP" I am just trying to understand who people are and what the business does. With each round of questions I get more specific, until I am sure I understand things well enough to draw conclusions.

What this methodology does best is help you realize when you are making assumptions. I guess I could have called this book "Assumption Busting." Although accurate, it's so ... boring.

Communication 101

Hopefully you have embraced everything I wrote in Section I and are now an excellent communicator. You can walk in a room, set people at ease, and talk to them about anything. So, what are you supposed to talk about? What should you ask? What should you say?

Who, What, When, Where, Why, and maybe How

I wish there was a perfect set of questions that I could use to solve every problem but there isn't. What you ask depends on what you are trying to do. I generally use the good old fashioned "Five W's." Who, What,

When, Where, and Why identify a lot of problems. Of course, I also like to ask How. Regardless of what you ask, what is really important is understanding the answer you get.

Who

Questions about "who" try to determine who is affected by the problem.

Think about my client who wanted a scanner to solve their paper issue. They called and asked if I could help select and install a server, scanner, and document management application. I started asking questions:

I ask: Who will use the scanner?

They reply: Me and my assistant.

I assume: This sounds like a small office.

I check my assumption: Who else works in your office?

They reply: Nobody. All other employees work remotely.

I assume there will only be a few employees scanning documents.

I check my assumption: How many remote employees are there?

They reply: One.

Assumption confirmed, this is a small office.

I assume they aren't about to hire a bunch of people.

I check my assumption: Do you plan on adding or reducing staff in the foreseeable future.

They reply: No. Assumption confirmed: This is a small office planning on remaining a small office.

I write down: Scanner would be used by two people.

When you get an answer from people, it is difficult not to take it literally. This client could have just as easily had 100 remote employees that also needed to scan documents, or could have been planning on hiring a whole new group of people.

The real trick to asking questions isn't the question, but realizing what assumptions you have made about the answers.

In this scenario, I have identified "Who" needs to manage documents.

What

Questions about "what" try to determine more about the process around the problem.

I ask: What documents need to be scanned?

They answer: Everything.

I assume: Bull, you won't scan junk mail, magazines, etc.

I also assume: Bull, it takes a lot of time to scan documents. You won't have time to scan everything.

I check my assumption: Can you give me examples of things you need to scan?

They reply: Contracts, photos, correspondence, invoices, bills, and other business related documents.

I write down the list of documents types they want to organize.

I think: I just read an article about courts and digital contracts. I'm not sure a court will accept a scanned copy of a contract in a lawsuit.

I recommend: You need to check with your lawyer to see if you can use scanned copies of contracts in the event you need one in court. They may require the original signature.

They reply: We want to scan them so we can find them easily but we will also file the original for legal purposes.

I assume: They must have a filing system for contracts.

I check my assumption: What do you do with contracts now?

They reply: They are in piles all over the office.

Assumption was wrong: They do not have a filing system for contracts.

I write down: They should check with a lawyer about scanning signed contracts.

At this point it seems clear they want to scan business-related documents into the system. Now I need to learn more about their current process in order to see how to fit document scanning into it.

I ask: How many contracts, invoices, bills, or other business related documents do you send or receive in an average week?

They reply: I have no idea.

I ask: How many contracts do you sign each year?

They reply: Maybe a dozen.

I ask: How often do you invoice them?

They reply: Monthly.

I assume there would be fewer than 144 invoices in a year if they send one a month to 12 clients.

I check my assumption: So you might send out 12 invoices in a month?

They reply: That sounds about right.

I write down: ~ 150 invoices per year.

I ask: How many bills do you receive a month?

They reply: ... after much thought ... about 10 invoices a month we have to pay.

I write down: ~ 150 bills per year.

I ask: How many photos do you take a month?

They reply: We have no idea.

I ask: When do you take photos?

They reply: at the beginning and end of each project.

I ask: How many photos do you take on average.

They reply: Maybe 20 per client.

I assume: 20 starting and 20 finishing photos for each of the 12 clients.

I confirm my assumption: So it sounds like you might take under 500 photos a year?

They reply: Yes.

I write down: ~ 500 photos per year. Confirm this later if possible.

I ask: How many other documents do you need to scan and store?

They reply: Not many. Just the occasional letter, legal document, etc.

I assume the volume is low.

I check my assumption: How many of these documents do you get a day?

They reply: Maybe one or two a week.

I write down: 10 additional documents per month.

At this point I am assuming the project is simple. They have about 50 documents a month that need to be scanned and archived. It almost seems like overkill for a company this small. In fact, I am wondering why a company with such a low volume of paper feels they need to spend thousands of dollars on a document management system.

I write down: Why do they need this?

If you don't understand why, ask.

You may not need to know and could be a waste of time but you could also learn something critically important.

When

Never forget the 4th dimension.

Time is a big deal. Time determines pace. Consider the document management project. Scanning 10 items a day is different than scanning 3,000 items in a week. Stop calling me Captain Obvious ... I'm not done. If my client wants to scan documents daily, the volume will be low but constant. If they wait until the end of the year, but have to scan them for some archival or legal reason, the volume would be huge but only for a short time. Pace is a major factor when researching the problem or solution.

When questions are all about timing, pace, volume, triggers, etc.

When do you do this?
How often do you do this?
How many times do you do this?

When do you know to start or stop doing this?

Continuing my interview with my client on the document management project ...

> *I ask: When do you file your bills or other documents that you want to start scanning?*
>
> *They reply: We don't. We just throw them in piles.*
>
> *I think: Why don't they file them now?*
>
> *I ask: Why don't you put them in files now?*
>
> *They answer: We don't have time.*
>
> *I think: If you don't have time to file, how will you have time to scan?*
>
> *I ask: If you don't have time to file, how will you have time to scan?*
>
> *They reply: ... wouldn't it be faster to scan than to file?*
>
> *I answer: No.*

This is the point in the project where I can tell I won't be eating again anytime soon. Time is the perceived problem. They don't have time to file. Replacing the filing task with a scanning task doesn't solve anything. The problem isn't where the document is stored, it is finding time to store the document.

You might also be noticing that I didn't ask questions about when they got their bills, when they got new contracts, etc. I got most of those answers when I asked them what and how much they scanned in the

"What" portion of the interview. In reality I would probably also ask when they got their mail, when they invoiced, etc. in order to determine the best time of day or day of the week to scan documents.

Now, back to the third dimension ...

Where

"Where" questions determine the location(s) of the "What." This is becoming an increasingly important question because we are becoming an increasingly mobile workforce. I am near Dallas, TX. I have a client now that is based in Minneapolis, MN. They have a client that I am helping as a subcontractor in Houston, TX. The systems I am working on are located all over the United States. There was a time when you could assume employees worked in an office. With so many people working from home or traveling and using mobile devices, those days are over.

"Where" isn't just about people. Where is about anything involved in the problem.

Where is the ...

- Document?
- Scanner?
- File Cabinet?
- Fax Machine?
- Printer?
- Accounting Department?
- Inventory?
- Customer?

"Where" is important because it affects so many things.

"Where" affects pace. It takes longer to do something when you have to go somewhere to do it.

> *I take my client's privacy very seriously. I shred all of my notes and documents when I am done with them. I have*

a shredder and it used to be about five feet from my desk. Because I had to move to the shredder to shred things, I created a "to be shredded" pile. It was common for this pile to grow so large it was probably violating OSHA safety standards. Once I moved the shredder to within arms' reach of my chair, I shredded things immediately.

Many problems can be solved by simply changing where something is.

"Where" affects access: An employee in one location doesn't have access to items in another location. Yes, again I am being Captain Obvious but this is often overlooked.

"Where" also affects culture. The culture in one office may be radically different from another office. This can be true for offices across the street or the country. When considering "where" don't assume everyone acts or reacts the same way in every location.

A client had a great culture and kept employees happy and engaged. They had weekly meetings which were more like parties where employees could talk about cool things that happened that week. They had spent years developing this culture and had very high employee morale. Then they opened a second office in another state. They tried to include the second location in all the corporate activities. Sadly, the second location ended up seeing what fun the first had and felt left out. Employee morale in the second location went down, and most of the employees left.

Just because it worked in one location doesn't mean it will work in every location.

Why

This is my favorite, and my client's least favorite, question. To be honest, I try to use it as little as possible. Asking someone "Why do you do that?" puts them on the defensive. I usually think "Why" questions and then translate them into "What" questions.

I think: Why the hell do you do that?
I ask: What are the business drivers for that process?

I think: Why didn't you change this insanely complex process earlier?
I ask: What prevents you from doing something different?

Why sounds accusatory. Use it wisely.

"Why" questions are in many ways the most important questions. People will stop and think about how they are doing things but they rarely have time for the more philosophical "Why." When I ask "why" questions, I am surprised at how many times I get non-answers like:

I don't know.
That's what I was told to do.
That's just the way we've always done it.

These are actually my favorite answers. They tell me people have been working on autopilot and have not considered the implications of doing what they are doing.

Non-answers almost always lead to the real problem.

When you get vague answers, spend extra time asking questions. You may find that people are doing things that simply don't need to be done anymore.

How

"How" is the politically correct way to ask "Why."

For example, send me an email telling me how you like this book. That sounds much better than "Why do you like this book?" To me, the why question implies you shouldn't like the book, whereas the how question implies you do like it. For my own self-serving purposes I would much rather imply that you like the book. I use the same methods when gathering information from people.

People love to talk about how they do things. They especially love to talk about how much they do, how busy they are, how irreplaceable they are, and in some cases how much like superman/woman they are. Although I make it sound like they are exaggerating, many times they are not. People do a lot of work and rarely get to brag about it.

Asking how things get done will help you fully understand how busy everyone is ... or is not.

> *One of my favorite techniques is to ask people how their proposed solution is going to help. Going back to my scanner client, "How will a scanner make things easier for you?" Sometimes the answer is dead on accurate. Other times it is an assumption like "It is faster to scan documents than put them in a filing cabinet." Either way, it lets me know what their assumptions are so I can research them.*

Listen for what is not being said

People don't always say what they think. People tend to keep important details to themselves when they are not comfortable disclosing them. This can prevent you from fully understanding the situation which prevents you from solving the real problem. People commonly omit information when:

- It makes their boss look bad.
- It makes themselves look bad.
- They are shy.
- They have been doing their job so long they operate on autopilot.
- They assume you know more than you do.
- They think the information you are asking for is confidential.
- They assume the information is obvious.

When you feel you are not getting all the information, keep asking questions. You may need to assure people that their answers are confidential. (Make sure they are if you do.) You can also have their boss assure them they can disclose all the details you ask for.

Learning to identify what is not being said is an art and one of the most difficult aspects of problem solving.

Retreat, regroup, and try again

When working on complex problems I often interview the same person more than once. The first series of interviews provide the general or high-level view of how things work. The next series allows me to get into the details. I find that when learning a new business or process, I may misunderstand what one person does because I don't yet understand the big picture. By doing short interviews first, I get an idea of how the entire process works before I try to understand the details.

There is a secondary benefit to this method. When I find someone is having trouble "spilling the beans" about a problem, I can hint about the fact that I have heard about the problem from others first. This almost always makes people feel better about telling me what is really going on.

Nobody likes being the first to complain, but if someone already has ... the floodgates open.

Taking notes

You are going to forget most of what people tell you.

I walk into every meeting with pen and paper. (For those of you in your 20's, that's what people used before computers.) Anytime somebody says something I want to remember, I write it down. I don't use sentences, I just write down enough to remind me what they said. Sometimes I draw pictures, flowcharts, graphs, lines, arrows, or whatever else will help me remember what people tell me. I use paper and pen because I can write or draw faster and more chaotically than most computer or tablet applications allow.

Note taking should not slow down the conversation.

Computers suck

I never use a laptop in meetings to take notes. There is nothing more distracting than the click-click-click of a keyboard. I can't easily draw lines, arrows, or other images and keep up with the conversation. Computers slow down the note-taking process, which disrupts the person giving you information, which results in frustration and confusion.

Tablets suck

I pre-ordered the original iPad. I buy every other model that comes out. I love the idea of having a small device which I can use like pen and paper. There are some great apps for the iPad, and I am sure for other devices as well, but they still don't allow me to write as fast and as randomly as I can with pen and paper. I really hope this changes in the future, but for now, old school still rules.

Recordings Suck

You might be tempted to just record what everyone says so you can review it later. Unless you are an unethical consultant that just wants to run your bill up, don't. For every hour of conversation you have, you will have an hour of recording to review. It is difficult and frustrating to review the recordings for that one nugget of information you though you heard but can't remember. Lastly, people tend to hold back what they are saying if they know they are being recorded, and recording them secretly is illegal in some states and unethical in all of them.

Transcriptions Suck

I am sure in a few years you will be able to put a computer in front of a group of people and have everyone's speech turned into neatly typed text in real time. Like recordings, that may not be a good idea. You don't need to remember every word of what was said. You need to remember the relevant details and what you thought about them at the time. Reading through a transcript is like sitting through the entire meeting again. That usually isn't very productive.

Whiteboards rule!

One of my favorite "technologies" for meetings is the old fashioned dry-erase whiteboard. I will use this more than pen and paper if I am having a group meeting. Everyone can see my notes and correct me when I misunderstand something. This is one of the most efficient ways of taking notes I have found.

Pictures rule!

When using a whiteboard, you will run out of space. I keep my phone out and when I need to erase the whiteboard, I take a few pictures. In the two seconds it took to snap a picture, I have recorded everything that was on the whiteboard. Most of the time, I email the pictures to myself, and sometimes the entire project team, for later use.

Paper Rules!

I know I said this before but there still isn't a more flexible medium than pen and paper. You can write or draw anything anywhere on the paper. Just remember that taking notes during meetings is about capturing information. Don't worry about making your notes pretty or organized, you are going to do that later.

My meeting toolkit

When I walk into a meeting I have a laptop bag. I pull out my laptop but don't turn it on. I pull out a pen and paper which I place in front of me. My camera phone, which is silenced, is placed to the left of my paper. I sit close to the whiteboard and have a bottle of water handy. I make sure I have dry erase markers that work and an eraser. I talk to people. I write down relevant facts. I take pictures of the whiteboard before I erase anything. The only time I use my computer is if they want me to see something online such as a file, website, or application.

The stealth technique

Sometimes people say things that are controversial. I don't always like to let people know when I write down something they just said. Consider the case where someone says something derogatory about someone else. If I grab my pen and write down "Bob thinks Sue is a $#@$!" it is going to destroy my ability to get information out of this person.

In cases where I want to remember something but don't want the other person to know I want to remember it, I simply wait to write it down. As soon as the topic changes, I grab my pen, and write down something vague to remind me what was said.

> *During an interview an employee was clearly uncomfortable telling me that her boss's daughter, who*

also worked at the company, was acting unprofessionally. Nobody wanted to be the one to tell their boss about this behavior. I didn't write any of this down at the time. As soon as we started talking about something else, I wrote down MY daughter's name. It was my way of reminding myself that the boss's daughter was causing problems for employees which needed to be addressed. The employee would have no way of knowing what that single name meant.

This technique isn't about lying to or deceiving the people you are talking to. It is about making them comfortable telling you things they might not normally tell someone. It is a way to deemphasize something they said so they will keep talking.

Research 101

You might be asking yourself – why don't I consider the entire process of problem solving research? Honestly, I do, but writing a book about the R methodology would be lame. When you are communicating with people, you are researching. When you are doing analysis, you are researching. Even when you are presenting your findings, you are researching how people feel about what you have discovered. The reason I created a step in my methodology called research is to remind myself, and you, to think about what you have learned and still need to learn before you draw conclusions.

Learning what you learned

For every hour I spend in meetings, I usually spend an hour learning what I learned. This is where I take my chaotic notes, pictures, and memories and compile them into legible notes. No more pen and paper. I start creating a document on my computer.

I use paper and pen to gather information and computers to organize and present it.

Almost everything is a process

Everything you do is a process. If I want coffee, I have to get up, ensure the coffee maker has water, turn it on, let it heat up, add a coffee packet, close the lid, put a cup in place, hit a button, wait, pick up the cup, blow on the coffee to cool it down, take a sip, savor, tale another sip, savor, etc. We don't think about this as a process because we know the steps and don't need to think about them.

> *A woman and her mother are cooking a roast. The woman cuts the ends of the roast and places it in a pan. The mother asks why she cut the ends off. The woman replies "Because you that's what you told me to do when I was a kid." The mother laughs and says she cut the ends off because she had a pan too small for the roast.*

Once we learn a process we tend to follow it without thinking.

The daughter in this story never asked why her mom cut the ends off her roasts. She just assumed that's what you were supposed to do.

Learn the entire process

When solving problems, it is important to understand the entire process around the problem.

> *My air conditioner repair man told me a story about a company his father worked at. They were creating heavy equipment for various government organizations. One of the requirements was to paint each piece of equipment a unique color so they were easily distinguishable from each other. They hired a troubleshooter after spending weeks and lots of money working with the paint department trying to*

figure out why the paint wasn't sticking to the metal equipment.

The troubleshooter started at the paint department and asked everyone what they did and why. He then went to the previous department in the assembly process and asked everyone there what they did and why. He did this until he came to a machinist that used a tap and die when manufacturing his part of the equipment. Part of his process was to cool the metal with oil while he was drilling. The oil would end up all over the equipment which he would wipe off as best he could before sending the item down the line.

The oil was keeping the paint from adhering to the metal. The problem was obvious once it was identified but because the employees had focused only on the paint department's portion of the process, they weren't able to figure things out.

Think of a process like a sentence. It would be really hard to understand if you were missing a bunch of letters.

When you are going through your meeting notes, you need to recreate the process as you understand it. As you do you will start to wonder why or how they do things. That will let you know what questions you still need to ask.

The excessive use of "why" is approved

I said previously that asking "why" can make people defensive. That is a semantic thing. I phrase my questions in ways that keep people talking. In my mind, though, I am asking why, why, why.

You should understand why every step in a process is necessary.

When nobody can provide a reason why a step is necessary, it can usually be eliminated. People do things, like cutting the ends off a roast, because that's the way they have always done it. They don't stop to consider how the steps can change when the environment changes.

Be cautious! There is no shortage of processes that are put in place for good reasons only to have the reasons forgotten over time. There is also no shortage of processes that are no longer helpful or necessary. It is difficult to tell the two apart.

The amount of research you do before eliminating a process should be proportional to the impact your changes could have on the business.

Rinse, wash, repeat

Pete and Repeat are in a boat. Pete falls out. Who's left? Repeat. Pete and Repeat are in a boat. Pete falls out. Who's left? Repeat. Pete and Repeat are in a boat. Pete falls out. Who's left? Repeat.

I usually go through multiple iterations of the communication and research steps before I am ready to draw conclusions. After every meeting I spend time looking up, validating, or learning more about anything I don't fully understand. For example:

I am often hired by a CEO, CIO, COO, or other high-level manager. They call me and want to know if I can do something. I ask them questions and schedule a meeting with them. I then think about what they told me, look at their company website and take a few notes. Communicate --> Research.

In our first meeting the CEO tells me what they think the problem and solution is. I ask a bunch of questions and then tell them who I need to meet with next. I then do a little research on their proposed solution. All this goes into my notes. Communicate --> Research.

Next, I meet with an employee and ask a bunch of questions. I find out what their portion of the process is and who else they interact with. I then update my notes and see if I need to talk to the other people involved in this process. Communicate --> Research.

I go back and meet with everyone again to get more details until I fully understand all the steps in the process and why each step is necessary ... or until the problem is, without assumptions, obvious.

Draw!

<Imagine old west gunfighters now>

You have asked questions until you understand everything you need to understand. You have taken time to review what you have been told ad research anything you don't understand. You should now be able to draw conclusions about what the real problem is. It is usually simple to document the problem at this point. The real fun is convincing the stakeholders you are right.

Analysis 101

In the Communication and Research phase of problem solving you are putting your client or company under the microscope. You are asking them why, why, why. You are forcing them to explain the value of their processes. In the Analysis and Presentation phases you are putting your own conclusions under the microscope. You are going to explain to them why, why, why your conclusions are correct. You are going to show the value of your services.

After answering "why" questions for hours, your clients will enjoy asking you "why" questions for hours. Be prepared.

Prove your point or else

I have had an air conditioning problem with both my upstairs and downstairs air conditioners for years. Every summer my upstairs starts to get hot. By the time it is 105 outside, a painful and un-rare event in the Dallas area, it is too hot to sleep, work, or breathe in the house. Every year I call the AC repair guys to come out and fix it. Every year there is a new "reason" why the problem comes back and keeps getting worse. None of these reasons explained what was happening. I knew it, I just couldn't prove it.

After trying several companies, I went back to the one I was less frustrated with and asked them to send their best troubleshooter. When he arrived he found that the builder had installed my compressors backwards, so the larger compressor was hooked up to the smaller indoor blower. Over the years, as the coils got dirty and less efficient, the larger outdoor unit started freezing the smaller indoor unit. This would cause the temperature to rise, which would keep the compressor running, which would keep everything frozen. That was the real problem!

I am upset with the companies that "fixed" the symptoms instead of working to find the real problem. I will not use them again nor recommend them to anyone.

Your clients will be able to tell if you are bullshitting them. Don't do it.

You must be able to explain to your stakeholders why something is a problem.

Start by defining the problem

Back to being Captain Obvious: Write down what you consider the problem to be. You should be able to do this in a sentence or two. Don't spend time writing a narrative that nobody reads anyway.

Be your client

Imagine telling your client what the problem is. Imagine they don't agree. How are you going to prove to them you are right? You need to think through the problem from their perspective to help prepare yourself for questions you will likely be asked.

People are emotionally tied to their jobs. Be prepared for an emotional response.

Walk through the process

Imagine walking them through the process. Show them how the problem starts and ends. Be prepared for "why" questions at every step.

Pete and Repeat

When I am analyzing the problem, or proving to myself that I really do understand it, I often go back to the client and talk about my findings and what I "think" the problem is. I am not presenting anything formal at this point but letting them know what I have found and why I think it is important. Many times they will ask questions or provide information which helps me document the problem or find a solution. Many times I start this process with the people doing the actual work and slowly move up to the managers, directors, or executives.

I commonly ask questions like "Can you think of anything else that might be causing this other than <whatever I came up with>?" This allows me to build credibility and camaraderie with those involved. This process usually makes the final presentation quick and easy.

Bulletproof

Your analysis is over when you can't find a way to disprove your findings. If you can't prove the problem exists, you will never be able to get approval to implement a solution.

Fuzzy Logic

Sometimes, you can't prove something. It is hard, for example, to prove a process is inefficient until you have changed it and seen the results. When faced with problems that cannot be proven, simply state that you can't prove it. It is common for me to tell clients that a process seems overly complex. I will provide examples of complexity and discuss how having a simpler process could help if one could be created.

Beware of mirrors

I was added to a project as a project manager a year after it started. The client was already displeased and ready to fire us. They were upset over technical problems we seemed unable to solve. We were frustrated because one person on their team would approve a change while another would deny it. We were essentially unable to implement fixes without weeks of debate.

It would been imprudent to say "Your employees disagree with each other at every opportunity, which is why we can't get anything done." Instead, I said there was a communication problem. I created a daily status report that went to the CIO showing what we requested, who was responsible for the task, and what the status was. Lastly, we promised that as long as they did what we requested, and our requests were reasonable, we would solve the problem in eight weeks or they wouldn't have to pay. (Our team was costing them $1,000/hour. That was a generous offer.)

After a week, not a single request we made had been approved or completed by their team. The CIO called a meeting ... that I was not invited to ... and by the end of the day, every task was complete. Two weeks later all the technical problems were resolved and the project was complete.

It would be easy for me to blame their internal disagreements for all the problems but I didn't. I couldn't answer the question I knew the CIO would ask, "Why didn't you tell us this sooner?" We were supposed to be highly experienced senior consultants. They had a reasonable expectation that we would bring problems to their attention before they spun out of control. Instead, we sat and watched them fight among themselves saying, "Not my problem." So, who was wrong? Everyone.

Pointing out flaws in someone else only encourages them to do the same to you.

In cases like this, I avoid pointing out other people's flaws. Instead of saying "Your team can't agree on anything!" I would say "Our team works better when we receive direction from one person on your team, such as the project manager." Even in the unlikely event you have never done anything wrong on a project, it is unwise to point out flaws in other people.

Finger pointing may win an argument but usually loses the war.

When people are the problem

Sometimes, someone is the problem. This is more rare than you might think. Most people think someone else is the problem until they understand why the other person does what they do. When you do encounter someone who is indeed the cause of a problem, be careful and be very sure of your findings. It isn't fun to watch someone get fired for something you found.

Be honest and fair

> *In my techie days, I always worried when someone said "My computer is slow." I cannot count the number of times I have found porn filling up their hard drive. It is easy to track who downloaded it, how long it has been there, etc. The employee violated the company's acceptable use policy by downloading porn. In every case, I was required to report the problem to their manager.*

When faced with a situation where someone is the problem, you need to be honest about it. When I found porn, I would tell the manager "I found pornography on Bob's computer." Notice I didn't say, "Bob has been surfing porn at work." The manager would ask if I was sure Bob was looking at porn and I would say that it was downloaded using his account, so either he did it or he gave his password to someone else that did it.

I never drew conclusions about what Bob was doing with the porn. I only confirmed that he had it and it violated policy. In cases where I wasn't sure how it got there, I would make sure the manager understood that I couldn't prove who downloaded it.

Porn situations are easy but it gets more complicated if you run into sexist or racist behavior. Stating that "Bob is a racist" draws a conclusion that might or might not be accurate. Stating that Bob makes comments that make other employees uncomfortable and violate HR policies lets the manager know of the problem without accusing someone of being something. Maybe Bob is a racist. Maybe Bob traveled through time from the 1840's and isn't aware of our social standards. It isn't up to me to judge Bob, I just need to identify the problem.

When in doubt, ask the expert

In these difficult situations, your friendly human resources manager is your best friend. Whenever I am trying to figure out how to deal with a people problem, I visit HR. If I am dealing with an accounting problem,

I ask an accountant. If I am worried the problem has legal ramifications, I ask a lawyer.

When a person is the problem, human resources is the solution.

Presentation 101

I don't like to present a solution until I have presented the problem. If your client or manager doesn't believe you have accurately diagnosed the problem, they won't buy into your solution. Conversely, it is easy to get a solution implemented if they clearly see the problem.

> *Although rare, I have had several clients in the last 15 years that would stop me while I was presenting a problem, saying something like "I don't want to focus on that right now." Instead, they want to focus on my proposed solution. This never went well because without understanding what was wrong, they couldn't understand why my solution was right. (Or good enough.) I don't necessarily walk away from these projects but I spend a lot more time documenting my recommendations so I can defend myself if the project goes bad.*

I cannot stress enough how important it is to keep the focus of any problem-solving project on the problem.

People love thinking about solutions but hate thinking about problems.

We get excited about solutions. We get excited about doing something new. We get lost in shiny new solutions and stop considering how or even if the "solution" solves the actual problem.

Stay away from discussions about solutions until the problem is well understood and accepted by all stakeholders.

Easier said than done

Did you hear the one about the employee that walked into a meeting and started talking about all the problems the company is facing? Probably not. The CEO found that by firing the employee, the problems were never heard of again. Okay, this is an extreme example, but executives and managers hate being told about problems. Since they are in charge of the company, it is almost like you are pointing out all their flaws.

One way to avoid this is to use problems as design specifications. Instead of saying "The problem is you don't have time to file your mail." we would say "We need a solution that makes it quick and easy to file mail." This may lead them to ask questions about why you need the solution. When they ask, you can talk at length about the problem.

Get buy in

People don't like going to meetings to learn about problems if they don't also learn about solutions. It is rare for me to have a formal meeting to discuss the problem alone. What usually happens is that I meet with stakeholders informally throughout the process to keep them up to date. At each of those meetings I talk about my findings. The real purpose of these meetings is for me to see if they understand and accept the problem.

When I feel the stakeholders agree what the problem is, I start thinking about solutions. If not, I keep doing working on communication, research, and analysis. Think of this as laying the foundation for your solution. If you do a poor job getting buy in, your solution will crumble later.

Telling people what they don't want to hear

Sometimes program changes hurt companies:

> *Your business will be bankrupt in two years. You are breaking even now. Changes in Medicare and Medicaid will reduce your revenue. You cannot lower your expenses and provide the same services you do now. If you continue doing what you do now, you will start losing money in one year and will be out of cash in 18-24 months.*

Sometimes bad luck hurts companies:

> *An equipment failure in one location is keeping the phones from working in every office in your organization. This equipment is old and cannot be repaired. It will take the phone company six weeks to install all the necessary phone lines for us to restore service. In the meantime, each location has only one phone to call out on and no way to receive calls.*

Sometimes ignorance hurts companie:

> *The database is corrupt and was not backed up properly. We cannot restore it. We will have to send the file to specialists, and they may or may not be able to recover all you data. It will take several weeks before we know the results.*

These are real comments I have made to real clients over the years. None them were happy about what I found. Bad news is bad news. Don't sugarcoat it. Don't avoid it. Don't apologize for what you find.

When telling people bad news, be honest, be quick, and be prepared for questions.

When it isn't funny to be funny

It is hot in my office. Both my air conditioners are broken. A company that I trust tells me I need to replace both units, which will cost me somewhere near $20,000. I don't know about you, but that is a lot of money to have to cough up unexpectedly.

When I told the air conditioner salesperson that I would be getting a second opinion before I spent that kind of money, his reply was "Good luck finding someone better. LOL. Just kidding ..." I like humor and use it all the time with clients, but there is a time to be funny and a time to be serious. How would you feel if your doctor walked in and said "You have cancer. Did you hear the one about the duck and a cowboy in a bar?" I took this comment as a challenge and found another company that was better AND less expensive.

Your client will want to be sure about your abilities, honesty, and integrity when you deliver bad news. Making jokes at a time like this is a quick way to lose clients, friends, or even a job.

When giving bad news, a little empathy goes a long way.

Make sure they understand the implications

When defining the problem, make sure everyone understand the implications.

> *I had an Enterprise Resource Planning (ERP) system fail once. All of the company's payroll, accounts receivable, accounts payable and much more was processed by this system. The real problem was that the system was broken and had to be replaced. The fact that the company couldn't pay its employees was something they had not thought of until I walked through what the system did and how long it would take to repair.*

You not only have to explain what the problem is, but how it affects the company.

Present, don't preach

Nobody likes a smart ass. Nobody likes to hear "I told you so." Nobody wants to hear "If you had only ..." Don't beat people up for what they could or should have done.

What's done is done. Let the experience do the teaching.

Most businesses learn from bad experiences, but some never do. You can't teach people what they don't want to learn.

> *I was asked to upgrade the domain controllers for a private company with offices in the US and Europe. This is one of those technical processes that if interrupted has the potential to be catastrophic. Right in the middle of the upgrade, the power went out. This was surprising since I was in a massive data center with backup generators and batteries. The battery backup system was old, had never been tested, and was broken. It took us two days to bring all their systems back online. (I had a contingency plan and my systems were back online in 15 minutes. Their other systems which I wasn't working on were the problem.) I estimate that they lost nearly $2,000,000 in revenue because they couldn't take or ship orders for two days. (They never disclosed their losses so that was nothing more than a guesstimate.)*

> *When I asked their IT director if they would like me to assist with disaster planning so things like this would be less likely, he told me the owner was an entrepreneur and risk taker. He would not be able to convince him to reduce risk. I couldn't understand it and to this day it*

bothers me, but they were perfectly happy continuing to operate that way.

You may have been hired to inform, not change.

You tell people what the problem is. You tell people how to solve it. They decide what they will or will not do.

Don't use adjectives

The completely unnecessary use of extraneous and overly descriptive text could be construed to confuse the very dedicated reader in completely unexpected and possibly unwanted ways. I strongly suggest using the absolute minimum number of descriptive terms such as adjectives and adverbs unless their use is completely and utterly necessary to make a very valid point.

The time it took you to read and comprehend the previous two overly complex and flowery sentences was a waste. I could have just said,

Keep it short

People aren't paying you to write a novel they don't want to read anyway. This is especially true if they are paying you by the hour. Your goal is to impress people with your ability to identify and solve problems which they have been unable to solve.

You have failed if you are trying to impress people with fancy presentations or lengthy prose.

If I have to present my findings to clients in writing, I keep my reports as short as possible. I keep my sentences as short as possible. I keep my words as short as possible. I will never win an award for writing, but my clients appreciate me not wasting their time and money.

Don't be overly simplistic

Just to be clear, being short and to the point is good. Being overly simplistic is bad.

> *Bob works at a company. The company is big. Sue is busy. Bob wants Sue to be less busy. Bob hired me to help Sue. Sue says she is busy and needs help. I agree. Bob needs to hire Sue help.*

The above report would and should get me fired. When I say keep it simple, I don't mean you should write like the reader is an idiot. The goal is to make your point clearly without wasting your client's time. Being overly simplistic doesn't make your point and may make people hostile.

Analogies

I love analogies. A good analogy is like a duck, it quacks when wet. If you understood that then I made a mistake. I use analogies when I talk to people. I don't use them often in my writing. I use them to make my point more clear, not less. The problem with analogies is that they only make sense to people that understand them. That may very well be the dumbest and most obvious sentence in this entire book. Let me waste less of your time by clarifying.

Hunting analogies only make sense to hunters. Animal analogies only make sense to animal enthusiasts. Child analogies only make sense to parents. College analogies only make sense to college graduates. Using analogies that don't make sense to your audience only confuses your audience. (Again with the super obvious points ... what a waste ... I'll pretend I am doing this to make a point.)

> *When explaining bandwidth to clients I usually say that an Internet connection is like a water pipe. It can only hold so much water. If everyone in the city turns their faucet on at the same time, there won't be enough water in the pipe, and only a trickle will come out of*

every faucet. That analogy makes perfect sense to me but doesn't to everyone.

I could say an Internet connection is like a garden hose and video is like a bowling ball. It would take a long time to suck the bowling ball through a garden hose. That analogy would be rather inappropriate regardless of how well it illustrates the point.

Analogies are dangerous, use them with caution.

Moving on

By now, you should have cycled through the CRAP methodology until all stakeholders fully understand and accept the real problem. This is a major achievement, the value of which should not be underestimated. It will be much easier to find and implement a solution now that all the groundwork has been laid.

PART III:
FINDING THE SOLUTION

Much of the time, my clients end up creating their own solutions to the problems I identify. Clients hire me when they have been unable to solve a problem. They have usually tried many solutions and failed. In most cases this is because they didn't correctly identify or understand the problem. Once I show them what is really going wrong, the solutions are often obvious. Perhaps I should call myself a problem identifier.

Problem solving is more about the problem than the solution.

Change your focus

While identifying the problem, your focus is usually internal and on your company, its processes, and employees. In this phase, you will be finding solutions. Many times, solutions come from outside vendors or experts. During this phase of problem solving, your focus will likely be outside the company. You may be looking at how other companies do things. You might look for new technology. You may just be remembering how you solved similar problems in the past. Your focus is now on finding a solution.

Stay current ...

When I meet with a new client, I don't like them to know more about my field than I do. In fact, it can be embarrassing when a client asks me about some new process or technology that I have never heard of. Since I prefer to avoid embarrassment, I spend an hour a day reading various blogs, tweets, and press releases. It isn't just that I like to know something about everything, it is part of what makes me valuable.

You could argue that experience is what makes you valuable. Experience tells us what has worked in the past and is all you need if nothing ever changes. Keeping up with current events makes us knowledgeable. When you can use your experience to apply new knowledge to old problems, you become invaluable. This is obvious in some professions:

- Accountants exploit new tax loopholes.
- Lawyers use new case law to guide their recommendations.
- Geeks find ways of preventing problems using new technology.

Regardless of your profession, continual learning and knowledge are keys to success.

If you aren't staying current in your field, you are falling behind.

... But not too current

You don't drown yourself when you are thirsty do you? That was a stupid question, how could you be reading this if you already drowned yourself?

Strangely, we know not to drown ourselves when we are thirsty, but when it comes to information we are perfectly happy drinking from the information fire hose called the Internet.

Read what you need. Ignore the rest. Don't get bogged down in irrelevant blogs, emails, or articles. I could write a book on information overload ... and I might one day ... but for now, I'll just say ...

Information overload is a symptom of your poor impulse control when it comes to information.

You don't have to check Facebook every hour. You don't have to respond to email the second it arrives. You don't have to check work email at home. You don't have to have your phone on you 24/7/365 so work can reach you ... unless it is in your contract. You don't have to follow every link someone sends you. You don't have to watch that funny video.

> ### *It is not only legal but a good idea to ignore much of what people think you need to read.*

Once again, read what you need. Ignore the rest.

Don't bleed to death

Have you heard about "cutting edge" technology? How about "bleeding edge?" Bleeding edge is the term we use to describe technology that is new and generally unproven. What I hate most about bleeding edge technology is that you never know if the company that built it will be in business in a few months. Imagine having a critical business process supported by some unproven untested technology and manufacturer that may or may not exist in a year. I just don't think it is good business in most cases.

Technology isn't the only thing with bleeding edge ideas. How many different management philosophies are out there? How about educational methods, ergonomic furniture, investment strategies, insurance products, and more?

> ### *Just because an idea is new doesn't make it good.*

When creating solutions, be careful what you recommend. Cutting edge can hurt and bleeding edge can kill.

Communication 201

The use of vendors is now approved

In Communication 101 you became an expert at communicating with the people that had the problem. Now it is time to communicate with the people that have the solution ... unless you know how to solve the problem yourself. Legal problems need lawyers, accounting problems need accountants, and technical problem need geeks. You can't be an expert on everything,

Don't solve problems you are not qualified to solve unless you can afford for the solution to fail.

I wish there was a magic formula for finding experts but there isn't. The simple fact is, some people are ethical and others aren't. It is hard to know who to trust.

Vendors, or salespeople for vendors, are great at finding solutions to problems you don't have.

Ask your peers

This is not an advertisement but when looking for experts, LinkedIn. com may be your best friend. I often go back through my contacts list to find people that work for companies similar to mine. I contact them to see if they can recommend a vendor or expert. I also look for contacts that work for vendors that might be able to help. If people you trust have a vendor they trust, that is a great place to start.

Beware of the Internet

Anyone can have an amazing website. Anyone can generate good reviews. For that matter, I have no doubt I could hire some spam company overseas to write great reviews of this book on every website where it is sold. People actually do this. (I don't; have you seen my website?)

The Internet is a great way to get misinformation.

Check their references

If you are going to hire a vendor or expert, check their references. If you are going to hire a vendor or expert, check their references. If you are going to hire a vendor or expert, check their references.

Sorry to annoy you with repetition but seriously, not checking references is just asking to be taken advantage of.

Be judgmental

It is rare to find a product or service that can't be purchased from more than one company. When you meet with a salesperson or consultant, if you don't feel good about them, don't hire them.

> *I was interviewing candidates for a server administrator position. My company was in a rural area and I didn't have a lot of highly qualified candidates for a high tech position. My last candidate to interview was the strongest technically. The initial interview went well and I was set to hire him. As I was walking him out, I showed him our server room. When he saw all the equipment, he said "Look at all the toys!" I didn't hire him. I didn't want someone to think about our critical systems as toys to be tinkered with. Those kinds of people tend to learn a lot at my expense. He could have been a great hire, but that one comment scared me off.*

When people don't do what they say, I run away.

> *I was a consultant at a company that was hiring salespeople. The sales manager would always walk the candidates back to their car after an interview. When I commented on how nobody ever walked me to my car after an interview, he told me he was looking to see what they drove. If the salesperson bragged of making million dollar sales every month but drove a 1972 Ford Pinto, he wouldn't hire them. I was appalled that someone would judge a candidate by what they drove. I'm still not sure*

it was completely ethical. Regardless, when people say one thing but their actions say another, you may want to steer clear.

When people can't demonstrate something, I run away.

While shopping for copy machines, I would ask the salespeople if the machines could do this or that, and they always answered "yes." When I asked them to demonstrate, and they couldn't, I moved on to another company. There are times when features can't be demonstrated and there are times when salespeople don't know what they are selling. If I can't tell the difference, I move on to a new salesperson.

When people don't listen, I run away.

When vendors are telling me about their solution, I listen carefully. I want to be sure of what I am purchasing. When I am telling them what I need their solution to do, and they are checking their phone or doing something other than paying attention to me, I end the meeting. If they aren't listening to me, then they cannot possible know what I need. Taking it a step further, I usually don't hire people that don't ask me smart questions after I tell them what I need.

There is a great book called "Blink" by Malcolm Gladwell, which talks about how our brains judge facial expressions that happen so fast we don't register them consciously. When talking to others, your brain may be picking up on facial expressions or body language which you do not see or understand. If you feel uncomfortable talking to someone, that may well be your brain telling you they aren't being as honest or straightforward as they sound.

One of my favorite sayings is "If you trust Google more than your doctor, it is time to get a new doctor." The same should be true of your consultants and vendors. If you don't trust them, don't hire them. You aren't required to explain to them why you don't hire them, so don't feel like you should.

I want to clarify one point. I am not saying it is acceptable to be racist, sexist, or any other "ist." I am telling you to trust your gut. If you feel you shouldn't trust someone, don't. If you don't trust someone because of race, religion, gender, accent, education, or some other bias that has nothing to do with competence, seek counseling or diversity training.

Being a translator

As a problem solver, you are often the middleman. You gather requirements from clients and communicate them back to vendors. You then take solutions from vendors and show clients how the solution would work in their specific situation.

Remember all that talk about assumptions?

> *A client was angry because a vendor had supplied copiers which they felt did not meet their written requirements. One requirement was that the copiers must be able to create transparencies for overhead projectors. The vendor said "yes." The client never asked anything more. They assumed they could keep using the same transparencies they had been using. The copiers could print to transparencies but they required a special type which cost three times more than what the client was currently using. In this case, I had to tell the client the vendor had delivered what they requested, and that their assumption about using the same transparencies was the problem. They didn't appreciate my conclusion.*

> *I did save the day, however. When I asked more questions I found that they were printing two copies of every PowerPoint slide for every presentation just in case a laptop died or was stolen. After a little math, I showed them that the transparencies cost over $10,000 per year. (They had a lot of PowerPoint slides.) For that price,*

they could buy a laptop and keep it on hand and ready to ship overnight if one was needed. They could also just buy a laptop at any retail store in the event of an emergency. The solution required little thought once I pointed out that they could buy five new laptops a year (or more) for what they were paying to print duplicates of their transparencies.

Don't regurgitate what one side tells you to the other. Spend time translating information into something that is easily understood by everyone.

If you are looking at technical solutions, you need to be able to describe it to non-technical people. Although technically true, "It uses ODBC to connect to your SQL system, processes data through multiple DTS configurations, and outputs the data using a web-service to CRM" is gibberish to most people. If a vendor told me that, I would tell my non-technical clients something like "Your accounting data will be imported into your Customer Relationship Management application using new software. We will have to use an expert to configure the data import so it works the way you want it to."

Being a referee

For a good time, sit in a meeting with the sales department and the accounting department and bring up expense reports. The sales team will launch into a diatribe about how difficult it is to get expense reports done, how long it takes to get paid, how many times they have to fix something, and much more. The accounting team will then talk angrily about how the sales staff doesn't understand company policy, basic accounting principles, regulatory compliance, and much more. In meetings like these, I regret not dressing like a referee and bringing both a penalty flag and a whistle.

In most cases I have found that both sides are right. Impossible, you say? Not really. The sales team is correct. Filling out expense reports is a pain, takes forever, and is often rejected when they do something incorrectly. The accounting team is correct that policy requires them to do things a certain way.

> ## *Instead of looking for who is most right or most wrong, figure out a way to help each side understand the other.*

In cases like this I will address the sales team and say "Look, nobody is going to just hand you a bunch of money and say 'Go spend it how you like.'" Then I look at the accounting team and say "If these guys can't wine and dine their customers, you won't be able to pay yourselves." I will then try to bring about mutual harmony by saying something like "We all want the same thing. We want the company to make money so we can make money."

Once people are reminded they are on the same team and depend on each other, they usually find a way to work together.

Experts make assumptions

After reading this book, you meticulously worked with your client to identify the real problem. Next you contacted an expert and explained the problem. The expert heard you through the ears of a person with years of experience. They immediately compared your problem to other problems they solved and created a solution based on past experience. That's great as long as the assumptions they made were correct.

> ## *Expert assumptions are rarely better than ignorant assumptions.*

When working with experts, vendors, or other solution providers, you have to ensure they aren't making assumptions. You have to make sure they have truly listened to the specifics of your problem.

My favorite technique to check vendor's assumptions is to ask them how they have solved similar problems in the past. What I want to hear from them is:

- They have worked on a similar problem before.
- They are thinking about a solution that might work for me.
- They are recognizing where their solution might not work in my specific case.

If I catch them telling me of a solution that will clearly not work in my specific case, I ask them to explain how it would be modified to meet my needs. If they can't, it may be time to find another vendor.

"I don't know." is great

I love vendors who say "I don't know." It makes me feel better about the expert's skill, honesty, and integrity. Experts don't know everything. (I hope that doesn't shock you.) In my mind, the best experts are the ones that know how to figure things out. They know where the best references are. They know where the best materials are. They have the right tools to test things that need to be tested.

Don't assume that "I don't know" means someone isn't an expert. It could mean just the opposite.

Don't be frustrated with experts that want to think about a solution, gather more information, or look something up. Conversely, I worry about experts that can pop off answers as fast as I can ask questions. I tend to find these walking dictionary types great at talk and lacking in walk.

Research 201

By now, you are the resident expert on the problem. Vendors are the experts on their solution. Your job now is to figure out which solution is good enough to solve your problem. We start by determining exactly what our solution must do.

Requirements

When documenting a problem, I usually create a list of requirements the solution must solve. This is common in the technology world but works well for most problems.

> *If we revisit my client that wanted a scanner and server to digitize all his paper documents, the requirements were:*
>
> - *Must be able to create digital copies of paper documents.*
> - *Must be able to digitize any size receipt or paper up to 11x17.*
> - *Must be able to digitize, name, save, and organize documents in less time than it takes to organize the original paper copies.*
> - *Must not cost more than hiring someone to organize paper documents part time.*
>
> *The first two requirements are easy. The second two were impossible.*

By having a clear list of requirements, it is easy to determine if a solution meets all your needs or not. This works for technical and non-technical problems equally well.

For example, here are a few requirements for a delivery vehicle:

- Must be able to haul 4,000 lbs.
- Must have a range of 400 miles on a single tank of gas.
- Must be able to hold three full pallets.
- Must be able to back up to a standard loading dock.
- Must be able to be loaded or unloaded with a pallet jack or fork lift.
- Must be enclosed but not climate controlled.

These requirements quickly rule out a pickup or van and leave us with a commercial panel truck of some kind.

Example requirements for a chair:

- Must be leather
- Must look expensive
- Must be inexpensive
- Must support 400 lbs.
- Must roll
- Must have lumbar support
- Must be ergonomic enough to keep employees from suing me

We may not get everything we want here, especially the part about being inexpensive, but you can see how requirements allow you to quickly communicate what you need to a vendor or search engine.

The must/like/wish rule

When looking over requirements it will be obvious that some requirements are more important than others. It can be helpful to implement the must/like/wish rule. Using the following rules, you label each requirement with Must Have, Like to Have, or Wish List.

Must Have: If the requirement cannot be met, the solution won't work. These are deal breakers.

Like to Have: You would really like this requirement to be met but will consider solutions without them.

Wish List: These are requirements you would like to have but can live without and are not be willing to pay extra for.

When given a list like this, I can provide clients with three prices. One that meets the "Must Have" requirements, one which also includes the "Like to Have" requirements, and one that includes everything.

Going back to our chair example we might apply the rule like this:

Requirements for a chair:

Must Have:
- Must support 400 lbs.
- Must roll
- Must be ergonomic enough to keep employees from suing me

Like To Have:
- leather
- expensive look
- lumbar support

Wish List:
- inexpensive

Based on this a vendor will know that the most important thing to you is staying out of court. The chair they recommend will almost certainly be different than what they would have recommended had they only seen the first list.

Know your limits

How much is it worth to solve this problem? Would you spend $10, $100, $1,000, or more? Is it worth spending an hour, day, week, month, or more on the solution? Does the solution have to be exactly correct in every way or can it be mostly correct? You need to have an idea of what your limits are before you start looking at solutions.

> *I used to customize and implement CRM applications. My clients wanted the best solution for the lowest possible price. I wanted to give them the best solution at a fair price. I needed to know their limits though. Were they expecting a $10,000 system or a $100,000 system? I could deliver either but the amount of customization and automation would be drastically different.*
>
> *I didn't want to demonstrate a $100,000 system for a client that can only spend $10,000. That would be like*

showing a Ferrari to someone that can only afford a Mazda. I didn't want to demonstrate a $10,000 system for a client that can spend $100,000. That would be like showing someone a Mazda when they are shopping for a Ferrari. In either case, the client would be disappointed.

The 4/40/400 rule

If you are working on a solution that is very complex, there may be hundreds or thousands of tasks associated with it. This is easy to understand in the software development world where one software customization project can contain hundreds of interface or field changes.

> *This rule is one I developed while consulting. We didn't talk in dollars but in hours. I would tell each client that we could meet each requirement with 4, 40, or 400 hours of programming. (The 40 is a normal work week thus the rule.) Since we were billing well over $100 per hour, the thought of a 400 hour solution for a single requirement was terrifying.*
>
> *This is a great way to demonstrate to your client or boss how easily a project can spiral out of control.*

Most solutions have many options. Not only do you have to choose if you will have a feature but also how complex that feature will be. You have to constantly ask yourself if you need that feature and if so, how valuable it is.

A great consultant will tell you when and why you shouldn't spend money on a solution.

> *When I felt my clients were wasting money customizing a Customer Relationship Management (CRM) in ways that would not benefit them, I would tell them. My stock phrase was "When a consultant that is billing you by the*

hour says to spend fewer hours on something, you should listen."

It might be an interesting exercise to ask your consultant for something that is clearly over the top. If they simply agree to go build it, look for a new consultant. Just as importantly, you need to be able to say no when the consultant shows you something shiny and cool but out of your original scope. When looking at solutions be honest not only about what you need but also about how elegant you need the solution to be.

What are your options

For any given problem there are lots of solutions. Ideally, you will be able to narrow them down to the ones that you can afford, implement in a decent time, and provide the level of perfection, accuracy, stability, etc. which is appropriate for your company.

So many options

If you wanted a new email system, there are thousands to choose from. Should you consider all of them? No. I look for the top two or three by reputation which also fit into my requirements and then choose. I only look at more when the top few solutions don't meet my needs.

When there are hundreds of essentially identical solutions on the market, find the top three and choose from among them.

So many options, part two

Unlike email, there are times when instead of hundreds of identical solutions there are hundreds of completely different solutions. Social Media marketing is an example. Do I use Twitter, Facebook, Foursquare, or something else to market this book? No, really, I want to know!?!? Each of these choices is different and requires consideration. In cases like this, I start with the service I am most familiar with and keep going through services until I have found the solution I am looking for.

When you have dozens of choices and you don't know which is best, start at the top and work your way down until you have a solution.

So many options, part three

Many choices, like email, can be broken down into categories. I could choose to host my own email system, have someone host a system dedicated to my company, or use a cloud service. If I were choosing a delivery truck I might think about vans, pickups, or panel trucks. Once I know what category to look into, I find the top two or three options and choose between them.

The dreaded one

<Imagine your worst nightmare here>

The only thing worse than having too many options is having only one option. Perhaps in a rural office there is only one phone company, one ISP, one electric company, one ... solution. The reason this is bad is that the one usually knows they are "The One." They price their services as if they are "The One." They assume, correctly, you will pay their exorbitant price because you have no choice.

Although I may be forced to hire "The One" now, there will come a day when competition arises and the one will become one of two.

To two or not to two

When the dreaded one has competition from the new two, it is very tempting to fire the one and hire the two. This may feel great but vengeance isn't always the best option. In this scenario, I always call the dreaded one and tell them I plan to switch to the new two unless they can meet or exceed the deal I just solicited from the two. Making the one grovel for my business is much more fulfilling than just firing them. It also prevents the pain of moving my business to a new vendor. Sometimes the one refuses. When they do, I still win because I get to fire them.

It's usually easier to ask your current vendor to lower their price than it is to change vendors.

Don't solve problems you don't have (yet)

When I am researching solutions, I often find solutions to problems I didn't even know I had. Worse yet, I find solution to problem that I think I might have ... one day. Or worse yet, solutions to problems that my solution might create. I have seen clients do this countless times.

If it's fixed, don't break it.

All solutions have unforeseen consequences. Another way of saying this is that you cannot completely predict how your changes will affect the company. Or you could say, the more you change, the less you will understand the effects of the change.

Solving problems that aren't problems is a problem.

Behold the power of the Internet!

I have a neighbor who is rebuilding a 1968 Trans Am. He told me he would have never made the oversized engine run if it hadn't been for Google. His exact words were "I Googled that shit." I'm not sure if using Google as a verb violates copyright, but I seriously want to print that saying on a t-shirt.

Most of the time, you can find a solution to what you need through the disciplined use of search engines. It isn't always easy, though.

Paid placement

All search engines allow advertisers to pay for placement. There are sections of Google's results that are organic, meaning Google thinks the website matches your search terms, and sections that include paid advertisements, meaning someone paid Google to put their ad on the page when anyone used those search terms. Many times the paid advertisements contain valuable links to relevant websites, but it is important to know the difference between the two. The top organic search result may be far more relevant than the best placed advertisement.

Advanced Search

Any researcher worth his salt knows how to do an Advanced Search on any of the major search engines. There are dozens, perhaps hundreds, of books on the subject, so I won't write another one here. If you don't know how to use many of the advanced search techniques available, learn them.

> *Much of my early career involved fixing misconfigured Microsoft servers. Although there were many websites that had good information, Microsoft's was the best. What was difficult was finding the information on the Microsoft website. At the time, Google did a better job searching the Microsoft site than Microsoft's own site search feature. When I needed to know something about an error on a server I would type something like "Windows 2008 error 10254 site:microsoft.com." The site directive at the end told Google I only wanted information from the Microsoft.com website. This drastically reduced the time it took me to find the information I needed.*

In most cases, someone has already solved the problem you are facing.

Don't recreate the wheel when you can steal.

No, don't literally steal, just reuse good ideas.

Ask for directions

One of the biggest complaints I get from clients, especially those that run their own small businesses, is that they feel like they work in a vacuum. They don't feel like they have anyone they can talk to about their company.

Working in isolation isn't a great way to grow professionally.

Once again, dig out your address book, contact list, or visit LinkedIn or other social networks, and look for people that you trust. Call them, write them, text them, eat lunch with them, drink with them, do something where you can have a conversation and talk about solutions. Even when my peers can't offer a solution, I find it helpful just to talk through the problem with them. Sometimes I solve the problem just listening to myself babble.

Pete and Repeat

When looking for solutions I go back and forth between the experts and my own research until I have one or more solutions I think might work. I prefer to have several solutions in mind at this stage. During the analysis phase I will determine the pros and cons of each solution and many times I end up eliminating several ideas.

Analysis 201

Believe it or not, all the hard work is done. All you have to do now is select the best solution for your specific situation. If you have a good requirements list and several possible solutions in mind, the rest is simple.

Being Analytical

- Does the UberTruck 2000 hold enough gas to travel 400 miles on a single tank?
- Does the UberTruck 2000 have a deck height which is standard for freight trucks?
- Can the UberTruck 2000 haul three full pallets?

Using your requirements, you can quickly verify a solution will work for you.

- Does the UberChair 400 roll?
- Is the UberChair 400 leather?
- Does the UberChair 400 look expensive?
- Is the UberChair 400 inexpensive?

Once you have identified several solutions that meet your needs, you are ready to present your findings to your client.

Is it really that simple?

No. Many requirements can be met literally, but not as the client intended.

- Can the copy machine print on transparencies? --> Yes (But at more than $3/sheet, it is cost prohibitive.)
- Can the UberTruck 2000 travel 400 miles on a single tank of gas? --> Yes (Empty, traveling downhill with a tail wind.)
- Does the UberChair 400 roll? -->Yes (As long as you aren't sitting in it.)
- Can that application be developed on budget and schedule? --> Yes (If you choose the least expensive and complex way to meet every requirement and never change your mind.)

Beware of buts

The hardest things to see when finding a solution is the but. It works but ... It is inexpensive but ... It is accurate but ... Buts can be disguised as excepts, ors, whens, and much more.

Looking for buts

The best way I have found to expose buts is to walk the solution through your specific process. This can be simple in the case of software. Have the vendor show you how to do every one of your requirements before you buy the software, for example:

- How do I create a new email account?
- How do I reset a password?
- How do I send an email?
- How do I find someone in my address book?
- How do I add someone to my address book?

When you find something that doesn't work the way you want, you may decide to abandon the solution and search for a better one.

It isn't always easy to see buts. Consider the UberTruck 2000's but:

Can it travel 400 miles on a single tank of gas? According to the vendor it can.

- We start the truck and back up to the loading dock.
- We load the truck. This takes time and the driver keeps the truck running.
- We drive up and down mountain roads all day.
- We often sit idle at client sites waiting for them to unload the truck.

Does this affect our fuel efficiency? Yes. Will this truck work? Maybe not.

The vendor told me so!

The last thing you want your boss to say is "The solution does not fit, you must quit." Replying with " but the vendor said ..." won't help much if you have wasted company time and money on a poor solution.

Don't trust vendors.

I don't hire vendors I don't trust to do things right. I trust them to tell me the truth. Regardless, I still check things out for myself whenever possible. This is especially true regarding any claim I read on a website.

Websites are developed by marketers. Marketers are paid to put the facts into the best possible light. Did you know your car can float* in the air? Sure it can. (* requires driving off a ramp at a precise speed putting the car into a parabolic arc which for a brief moment will allow the car to float shortly before it crashes into the ground causing catastrophic structural failure.) Now that's marketing!

When Microsoft introduced a new service to help manage PCs, they had a claim on their website saying you could save $500 per PC per year by using their new service. The white paper used to support this claim was lengthy and took into account costs which the average small business will never have. They have since taken this claim down, but it made for great blog fodder for a while.

When reading websites, I mentally add "in the right circumstances" to every claim made.

Testing can be fun! (in the right circumstances)

Testing is the one way to make sure a solution works. Testing is also the one thing companies either do half-ass or not at all. If you catch yourself assuming something will work, start assuming it won't.

Solutions are just theories until they have been tested.

Large solutions require large testing efforts.

Sign this

One way to ensure that people will test a solution is it to hold them accountable. You can do this by putting all the requirements a stakeholder is responsible for in a document. Make them sign sign off that the solution meets the requirements. If they sign it, they are then responsible if something doesn't work. In my experience, people won't test thoroughly unless they know they will be held accountable at the end of the project.

Test this

You need to test each and every requirement. Then you need to test the solution as a whole. Going back to the UberChair 400, it is easy to test whether it rolls. You push the chair across the room. Behold, the chair rolls. The requirement has been met. That is testing an individual requirement. It isn't until you put the chair at a desk, sit in it, and try to roll over to the paper shredder that you realize the chair doesn't roll when fully loaded.

Testing the entire process around the solution can uncover failures that might not show up when testing each specific requirement.

I am sure there are solutions out there that don't need to be tested but they are far and few between. Not testing a solution is far more likely to contribute to failure than testing will.

You don't have to test every solution but you should think about testing every solution. Make an informed decision.

Don't create more work

Most people are already working full time. Creating more work for them is generally not appreciated. (I should win an award for understatement.) Unless you have a bunch of underutilized employees, you cannot create a solution that creates more work. There simply isn't time for them to do more. For each new task I create, I find another to eliminate. I pay careful attention to how long the new process takes compared to doing things the old way.

Many of the problems I solve are due to people overcomplicating things. When I simplify a process, it is usually more efficient. In the rare event I have to add tasks to a process in order to solve a problem, I also have to consider hiring more employees to do the work.

Shuffle cards, not jobs

A common problem I find is that when one employee gets too busy, the manager just shovels some of the work onto another employee ... which makes that person too busy ... so the manager shuffles some of the work to yet another employee ... and that employee gets too busy ... and so on.

It is acceptable to have one employee help another out in a crisis, but if you are regularly shuffling tasks between employees, you are the problem.

Moving tasks between employees is rarely a permanent or efficient solution.

ROI, TCO, and other bull

Your client will want to know how much your solution will cost to implement, maintain, replace, etc. They will want to know what they will save or spend. They will want to know what risks they are mitigating. They will want to know the cost benefit of your solution.

Vendors are VERY helpful with cost benefits. Many have online ROI (Return on Investment) calculators, TCO (Total Cost of Ownership) spreadsheets or other tools they are happy to provide so you can show your boss how much they will save by spending money.

Most of the calculators I have used show that I will save more than I am currently spending if I just spend more. That only makes sense in bizzaro-world.

Return on Investment, Total Cost of Ownership, and other calculations have merit but can be severely abused. It's a little like the saying "There are three types of lies: lies, damn lies, and statistics." That's how I feel about most ROI or TCO calculations.

If you can't prove it, don't use it.

As a general rule, I try to overestimate my costs, overestimate the time-line, and underestimate functionality. If I can sell a solution using those handicaps, I will almost certainly over-deliver ahead of schedule and on budget.

People will like you more if you over-deliver.

Real Benefits

Some benefits to a solution cannot be easily quantified. How much will we save by making people more efficient and less stressed? Who knows, but it is a benefit worthy of mentioning. Instead of placing a dollar value on unknowns like efficiency, list them as a benefit.

"The UberTruck 2000 has a great air conditioner at no additional cost to us, which keeps our Texas drivers cool and happy." That is a benefit with little or no quantifiable value.

Go out on a limb

Which solution do you recommend? You have analyzed several. You are the only person that understands all the issues involved. This is perhaps the hardest part of the process, making the final decision. You have to avoid analysis paralysis. You can't pass the buck because nobody else understands all the facts. It is time. Make the call.

Let's get ready to rumble!

If you have followed some of the advice in this book, you have identified:

• The real problem
• All the processes and people involved in the problem

- Requirements to solve the problem
- One or more solutions
- How well each solution fulfills the requirements
- The costs and benefits of each solution
- Your recommended solution

You have everything you need to confidently present your solution to your boss or client.

Presentation 201

You are sitting in a room full of people. Perhaps you have a laptop and projector showing slides with fancy facts and figures. Everyone has their coffee in one hand and cell phone in the other, texting each other across the table. It is time to wow them.

Do it your way.

I hate PowerPoint. I hate sitting through meetings watching PowerPoint. I hate presenting using PowerPoint. There are others that agree with me and yet more that don't. I only use PowerPoint when I need to show people things that I cannot describe very well, such as screenshots of applications, graphs, pictures, etc.

Other presenters use PowerPoint effectively. They have awesome slides, speak from notes so they don't repeat what is on the slide, and have clear layouts, graphics, and style.

Some people, like me, pace when they present. I just think better on my feet. Some people sit in a chair and drive a computer running the on-screen display. Some people make jokes while others are deadly serious.

When it comes time to do your presentation, be yourself. There is nothing worse than a dry person trying to be funny, or a funny person trying to be serious. They end up sounding fake through the entire presentation.

This is the time to sound, and to be, honest.

However you choose to present your findings, do it in a way that is comfortable for you.

Don't do it your way

OK, I lied. There is one thing worse than a presenter trying to present something in a style that isn't their own. It is a presenter trying to present something in a style or format their client hates. If your CEO is serious, have a serious presentation. If your managers like humor, try to throw in a few funny slides or jokes. If they expect PowerPoint, use it.

Balance your client's expectations and your style.

The agenda

It is a good idea to have an agenda for meetings. They keep people focused and let them know why they are confined to a chair. This is an example of an agenda I might use:

Today we will

- Review the problem
- Review the processes and people involved
- Briefly discuss the requirements for a solution
- Discuss my recommended solution including costs and benefits
- Discuss other possible solutions if necessary
- Make a decision or schedule when the decision will be made

Review the problem

Be quick. People should have already seen this information. Don't go back through all of what you did in Presentation 101. Just cover the problem at a high level and move on.

Review the processes and people involved

This should also be short and not a repeat of Presentation 101. This is to remind people what is at stake and who is going to be hurt by their failure to solve the problem.

Discuss the requirements

If this is a simple project with only a few requirements then I would discuss each. If there are hundreds or thousands of requirements, I would provide them in a separate document and only discuss them at a high level. When I was working on software projects I would break down the requirements into categories such as Interface, Data Storage, Back End, etc.

The goal is to make people understand what the solution must do.

Present the recommended solution

Hey, you wanted to be a problem solver. That's why you are reading this. Time to put your mouth where their money is. Tell them what you think the best course of action is and why. I try to avoid showing them how the solution meets each requirement unless they just want to see it.

By this time, you should know your audience. You have worked with them for days, weeks, or more. You should know if they want the details or just an overview. Give them what they want but be careful with the details.

I have seen meetings completely derailed over some trivial detail. We could be talking about a million dollar application and someone spends 30 minutes talking about screen colors. We could be talking about supplying bran muffins in the break room and someone would argue about how that would increase toilet paper costs. Seriously, some people go to meetings looking for things to debate. Try to stay above it.

When people try to derail a meeting by arguing the small points, I ask them to review the report and if they feel there was an error, to let me know. Of course that means I have to have a report with all my calculations in it ready to give them. Other times I will tell them that I could have calculated the extra cost of toilet paper but was sure that the cost of my time for doing the calculations would exceed the cost of toilet paper. "I'll be happy to consider that if you feel it is cost effective."

These are opportunities to teach "Good Enough."

Discuss the other solutions if wanted

This is where I show the other solutions I considered and why I didn't recommend them. This is what really sells your initial recommendation. If the client sees that you have done a thorough job of evaluating the available options, they will be more comfortable with your recommended solution.

Decide to decide

If you can't get the client to decide to implement the solution in this meeting, schedule another meeting then and there. If you don't, nobody will think about the issue again. If you have made it this far in the process, it is important that you keep the momentum moving forward.

What's next?

At this point, you have theoretically solved the problem. You won't know if the solution works until you get it implemented. That should be easy right? <Imagine maniacal laughter from the author here.> The good news is that the problem has moved from the domain of problem solver to the domain of project manager.

I hate project management.

I have found most project management techniques heavy on management and light on getting things done. Since nothing in the title of this book implies I will discuss project management, I will save that rant for another time, book, or blog entry.

With any luck, you can hand off the project management to someone else and find another problem to solve. If not, get the solution implemented and bask in the glory of your accomplishments.

The Art of Problem Solving

It isn't that I don't like education. I used to be a school teacher. My wife is a professor. I have a master's degree. It's just that I don't think school prepares you for the real world. Schools teach you science. The real world teaches you art.

There is a science to management. There is an art to management. There is a science to project management. There is an art to project management. There is a science and an art to everything.

It took me 15 years to realize that I wasn't especially skilled in the science of problem solving, management, or technology. Instead, I was skilled in the art of it. The science teaches a methodical way to approach things. The science of management and problem solving works great when people are perfectly rational ... which they never are. (See Predictably Irrational by Dan Ariely. Harper Perennial; 2010) The art of problem solving takes into account the fact that people have fears, compromise is necessary, perfection doesn't exist, etc.

The science of problem solving is a process which can be set in stone. The art of problem solving requires you to adjust your approach based on how people think and feel.

By now it should be clear that I solve problems by working with people. I listen to them. I repeat what I have learned back to them. I watch for the assumptions we all make. I look for balance in all things. I don't look for the perfect solution, I look for the right solution. This is obviously not a methodology taught in school but one learned from 15 years of hard experience, success, failure, and everything in between.

I sincerely hope this will help you solve a problem. If you get a chance, visit my website (Decomplexification.com) and tell me what you liked, or didn't like about this book. Let me know how it did or didn't help you. Tell me about problems you have solved using the memorably named CRAP methodology. Even better, tell me how you have improved on my ideas.

Thanks for reading this book. It was fun to write and I hope, fun to read.

Bryan

www.ingramcontent.com/pod-product-compliance
Lightning Source LLC
Chambersburg PA
CBHW051333170526
45166CB00002B/797